introduction

Gardens and gardening mean different things to different people. For some they're an exercise in harmony with gentle nature, working with indigenous plantings and fostering supportive habitats for native birds, insects and wildlife. For others they become a test of will and technology versus nature untamed – the besieged human species struggling valiantly to bring order and discipline to the forces of anarchy and chaos. One garden might have beds and planting areas that seem to be scattered randomly across the landscape, while in another they are laid out with laser-like, geometric precision.

I admit to at least a nodding acquaintance with both philosophies. As a cabinetmaker, I subscribe to the ideals of careful layout, precise measurement and accurate execution; but I can also appreciate soft lines, meandering borders and the occasional item that seems to make absolutely no sense the first time you look at it. In our own garden, my wife and I have tried to utilize both approaches. Some areas we have planned with some formality, while some we have consciously left a bit wild and unruly. Also, being a woodworker, the planning occasionally drifted in a direction that just might involve a bit of carpentry.

The projects presented in this book are the result of the ongoing head scratching and problem-solving that make up a good part of gardening and landscaping. For each one I have tried to give an idea of what – be it problem or opportunity – we were dealing with, what we decided to do about it and how the decision was carried out. I've shown the planning, design and building process for each project. But this is not really a "project" book. What was right for my space and situation obviously won't work for everyone and shouldn't. Instead, I hope the reader will take away some of the ideas and procedures presented here to consider, modify, improve and expand upon – and then apply them to his or her own garden in the future.

Have fun!

John Marckworth

Beautiful
Wooden Projects
for Outdoor Living

JOHN MARCKWORTH

POPULAR WOODWORKING BOOKS
CINCINNATI, OHIO
www.popularwoodworking.com

Read This Important Safety Notice

To prevent accidents, keep safety in mind while you work. Use the safety guards installed on power equipment; they are for your protection. When working on power equipment, keep fingers away from saw blades, wear safety goggles to prevent injuries from flying wood chips and sawdust, wear hearing protectors, and consider installing a dust vacuum to reduce the amount of airborne sawdust in your woodshop. Don't wear loose clothing, such as neckties or shirts with loose sleeves, or jewelry, such as rings, necklaces or bracelets, when working on power equipment. Tie back long hair to prevent it from getting caught in your equipment. People who are sensitive to certain chemicals should check the chemical content of any product before using it. The authors and editors who compiled this book have tried to make the contents as accurate and correct as possible. Plans, illustrations, photographs and text have been carefully checked. All instructions, plans and projects should be carefully read, studied and understood before beginning construction. Due to the variability of local conditions, construction materials, skill levels, etc., neither the author nor Popular Woodworking Books assumes any responsibility for any accidents, injuries, damages or other losses incurred resulting from the material presented in this book. Prices listed for supplies and equipment were current at the time of publication and are subject to change. Glass shelving should have all edges polished and must be tempered. Untempered glass shelves may shatter and can cause serious bodily injury. Tempered shelves are very strong and if they break will just crumble, minimizing personal injury.

Metric Conversion Chart

to convert	to	multiply by
Inches	Centimeters	2.54
Centimeters	Inches	0.39
Feet	Centimeters	30.5
Centimeters	Feet	0.03
Yards	Meters	0.91
Meters	Yards	1.09

Distributed in Canada by Fraser Direct
100 Armstrong Avenue
Georgetown, Ontario L7G 5S4
Canada

Distributed in the U.K. and Europe by David & Charles
Brunel House
Newton Abbot
Devon TQ12 4PU
England
Tel: (+44) 1626 323200
Fax: (+44) 1626 323319
E-mail: mail@davidandcharles.co.uk

Distributed in Australia by Capricorn Link
P.O. Box 704
Windsor, NSW 2756
Australia

Visit our Web site at www.popularwoodworking.com for information on more resources for woodworkers.

Other fine Popular Woodworking Books are available from your local bookstore or direct from the publisher.

10   09   08   07   06   5   4   3   2   1

Library of Congress Cataloging-in-Publication Data

Marckworth, John.
    Beautiful wooden projects for outdoor living / John Marckworth.
       p.   cm.
    Includes index.
    ISBN-13: 978-1-55870-772-6 (pbk.: alk. paper)
    ISBN-10: 1-55870-772-7 (pbk.: alk. paper)
    1. Outdoor furniture--Design and construction.   2. Garden ornaments and furniture--Design and construction.   3. Woodwork.   I. Title.
TT197.5.O9M36   2006
684.1'8--dc22   2006008276

ACQUISITIONS EDITOR: Jim Stack
EDITOR: Amy Hattersley
DESIGNER: Brian Roeth
ILLUSTRATOR: Len Churchill
PRODUCTION COORDINATOR: Jennifer L. Wagner
PROJECT OPENER PHOTOGRAPHER: Craig Wester
STEP-BY-STEP PHOTOGRAPHER: John Marckworth

(dedication)

To Phyllis, my tour guide into the world of the garden. You point and I'll dig!

About the Author

John Marckworth has worked as a carpenter and cabinetmaker for the last twenty-five years. He owns and operates Marckworth Specialty Woodworking in Port Townsend, WA. His business card reads, "Furniture, Custom Cabinetry, Fine Finish Carpentry and Interesting Projects" and he enjoys them all.

John, his wife Phyllis and their daughter Kate are also avid gardeners and have spent many years turning a back yard full of six-foot-tall blackberry bushes into the garden for which the projects in this book were designed.

He plans additional garden projects in the future and may even get around to mowing the lawn.

Acknowledgements

My heartfelt thanks to all who helped make this book possible:

To Phyllis, who is still patiently waiting for me to finish the kitchen remodel.

To Kate, who grew up with the whine of the tablesaw in the background, insisting that it really didn't bother her...

To Bob Schwiesow and Anne Hirondelle, who showed me that new careers are possible and that remodeling can be fun.

To Jim Tolpin – author, woodworker and friend – who recruited me into the world of writing about woodworking.

To Craig Wester – photographer extrodinaire.

To all the woodworkerss who have so generously shared their knowledge and tips over the years.

And finally,

To Jim Stack and Amy Hattersley – my editors at Popular Woodworking Books – who have led (not to say herded) me through the process with good humor, help and support. And to the rest of the staff at F+W Publications.

Len Churchill – your artwork is the best.

(table of contents)

introduction...6 • suppliers...126 • index...127

1 Adirondack-style fanback loveseat...8

2 bench seats and table...22

3 garden fence with door...34

4 potting bench...48

5 covered BBQ station...58

6 wooden walkway...72

7 tool shed...80

8 trellis with paving stones...94

Adirondack-style fanback loveseat

1

Say the words, Adirondack chair and your mind immediately conjures up an image of pure relaxation. This traditional wooden slat design with wide arms and comfortably slanted back and seat can be traced to the upscale resort hotels and vacation homes of the Adirondack mountain region of upstate New York during the late 19th and early 20th centuries. The chair has maintained its popularity and today is considered an American classic.

One reason the basic design has remained popular is that it lends itself to experimentation and modification. I wanted a loveseat that would provide comfortable seating for two with a pleasing design and some simple elegance. By combining old and new elements from the many Adirondack-style chairs and loveseats I've seen over the years, I was able to develop a design that met my needs. I made the fan back a bit higher and wider than most and made the arms wider to provide enough room for a glass and a small plate. The seat is fairly low to the ground and, in combination with the rounded seat front, provides a comfortable leg extension without the need for a footrest.

Choosing materials for outdoor furniture is a process that involves considerations of durability, weight, joinery techniques and aesthetics. Teak is a traditional wood of choice because of its superior weathering qualities, while cedars are lighter and less expensive (although less durable). I chose to use Alaska yellow cedar for the loveseat frame components and ipe — a tropical hardwood often used for high-end decking — for the slat arms, seat and back. This combination provides a nice contrast of wood colors and grain which can either be maintained with an exterior oil sealer or left to weather naturally to gray.

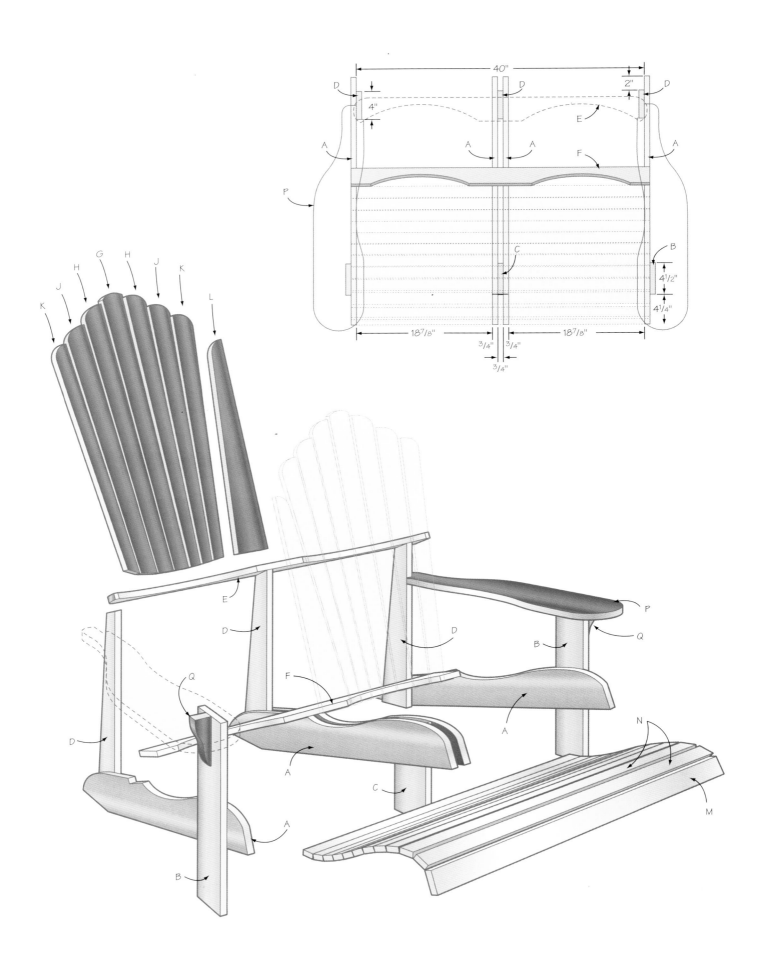

inches (millimeters)

REFERENCE	QUANTITY	PART	STOCK	THICKNESS	(mm)	WIDTH	(mm)	LENGTH	(mm)	COMMENTS
A	4	seat support frames	redwood*	3/4	(19)	5 1/4	(133)	36 1/2	(927)	
B	2	front outside vertical frames	redwood*	3/4	(19)	4 1/2	(115)	24 1/4	(616)	
C	1	front center vertical frame	redwood*	3/4	(19)	4 1/2	(115)	12 1/4	(311)	
D	3	rear vertical frames	redwood*	3/4	(19)	4	(102)	26 1/4	(666)	tapered with angled top cut
E	1	upper back support frame	redwood*	1	(25)	3 1/2	(89)	40 3/4	(1035)	
F	1	lower back support frame	redwood*	1	(25)	3	(76)	41 1/2	(1054)	
G	2	center seat back slats	ipe	3/4	(19)	2 3/4	(70)	36 7/8	(936)	tapered with shaped top
H	4	seat back slats #2	ipe	3/4	(19)	2 5/8	(67)	35 5/8	(905)	tapered with shaped top
J	4	seat back slats #3	ipe	3/4	(19)	2 5/8	(67)	33 3/8	(848)	tapered with shaped top
K	4	seat back slats #4	ipe	3/4	(19)	2 1/2	(64)	31 1/8	(790)	tapered with shaped top
L	2	seat back center spacers	ipe	3/4	(19)	4 1/4	(108)	28 1/4	(717)	tapered with shaped top
M	1	first seat slat	ipe	3/4	(19)	2 3/4	(70)	41 7/16	(1052)	
N	11	seat slats	ipe	3/4	(19)	1 11/16	(43)	41 7/16	(1052)	
P	2	arms	ipe	1	(25)	7	(178)	32 3/8	(823)	glue/assemble if necessary to achieve width
Q	2	arm supports	ipe	1	(25)	3 1/2	(89)	8	(203)	

*I used Alaska yellow cedar but redwood is more readily available.

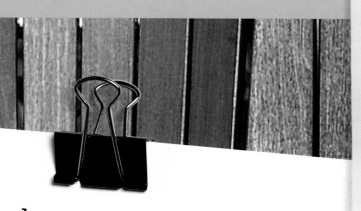

hardware and supplies

1/4 (6mm) - 20 × 3" (75mm) silicone bronze carriage bolts

1/4 (6mm) - 20 silicone bronze hex nuts

1/4" (6mm) silicone bronze flat washers

1/4" (6mm) silicone bronze split-ring lock washers

No. 8 × 1 1/4" (30mm) silicone bronze flathead screws

TECH tip
fastening in hardwoods

Using mechanical fasteners in hardwoods (and especially in super-hard woods such as ipe) requires heads-up planning and some special techniques. Predrilling is a must or a split board or even a broken-off screw can easily result. Examine the grain carefully for defects or checking before driving a fastener.

The Frame: Build From the Ground Up

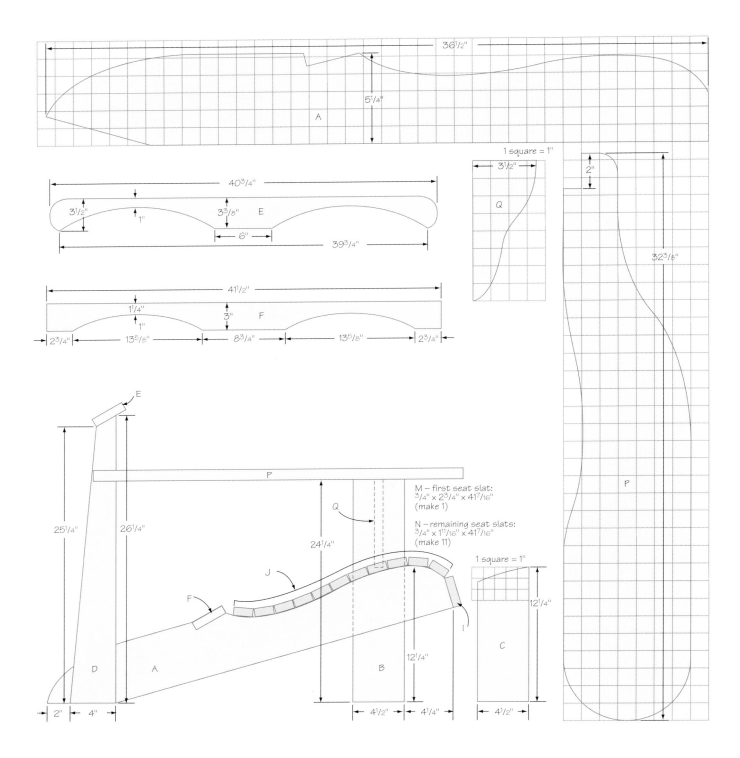

1 square = 1"

M – first seat slat:
3/4" x 2 3/4" x 41 7/16"
(make 1)

N – remaining seat slats:
3/4" x 1 11/16" x 41 7/16"
(make 11)

1 square = 1"

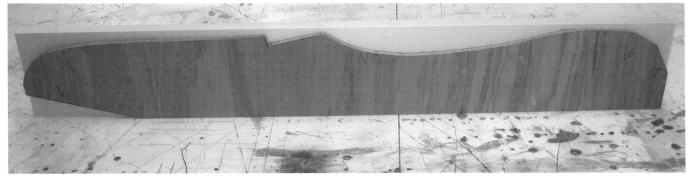

1 The four seat support frame pieces are exactly the same, so one pattern is all that's required. I made it from a piece of ¹/₂" (13mm) plywood, following the scale/grid layout dimensions. Note the flattened face on the front of the piece where the first few seat slats will be attached.

2 The plywood pattern functions as a shaping guide. First, attach the pattern to the board with small brads (extra strength, double-sided carpet tape could also be used). Next, cut to within an ¹/₈" (3mm) of the edge of the pattern with a jigsaw or band saw. After firmly clamping the piece to a work surface, trim the excess material to the pattern outline using a straight-cutting router bit with a pattern guide bearing. Do this for all four pieces.

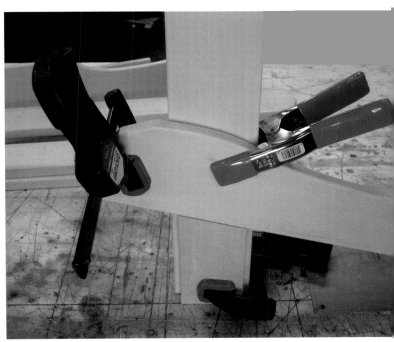

3 Make a spacer block that fits against the vertical frame piece below the seat support piece and clamp it in place. This helps to support and stabilize the seat support piece during assembly and will also serve as a location guide for assembling the other front vertical frame pieces.

Possible Fasteners

Attaching the seat supports to the vertical frame pieces needs to be done correctly, since this assembly provides the major support for the entire structure. I chose to use Alaska yellow cedar — a relatively soft wood — for the frame, so I needed to be sure that the connectors were solid and wouldn't work loose over time with the pressures, racking and torque experienced in everyday use. I considered screws, but in the end decided on marine-grade silicone bronze carriage bolts, washers, split lock ring washers and nuts. These provide good holding power and fewer are required than screws.

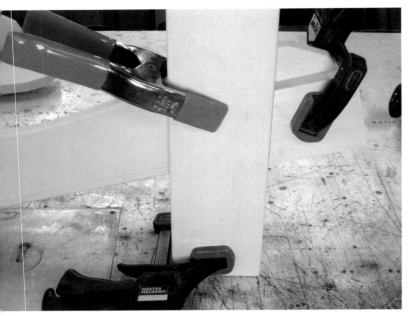

4 Make a block that fits between the front vertical edge and the front end of the seat support piece and clamp it in place. This will provide support and stability during assembly and serve as a location guide for assembling the other front vertical frame pieces.

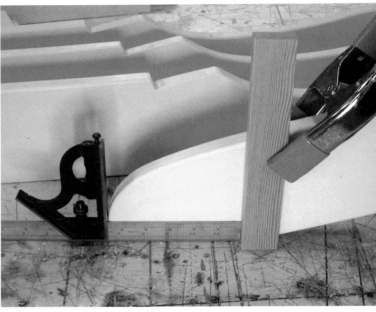

5 Measure the setback from the inside back ends of the right and left seat support pieces, then clamp a block in place on each square to the work surface.

6 Set the straight (untapered) front edge of the right and left rear vertical frame pieces in place, against the locator blocks and square to the work surface. Then clamp them in place.

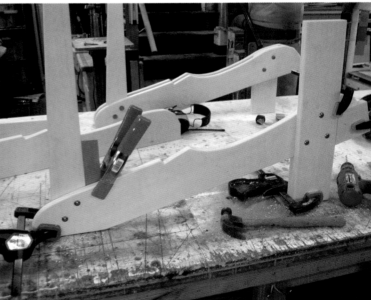

7 Once the right and left frame sections are firmly clamped in place, fasten them together with the carriage bolts.

8 Using the blocks you made for the right and left front vertical frame pieces, position the center front vertical frame piece on one of the two center seat support pieces, making sure that the flat foot at the rear of the piece is resting flat on the work surface. Clamp the vertical in place and attach it with two small brad nails.

9 The center rear vertical frame piece is positioned exactly the same as the right and left rear vertical frame pieces. Using the same layout measurement and clamped block, position and clamp it in place and attach it using two small brad nails.

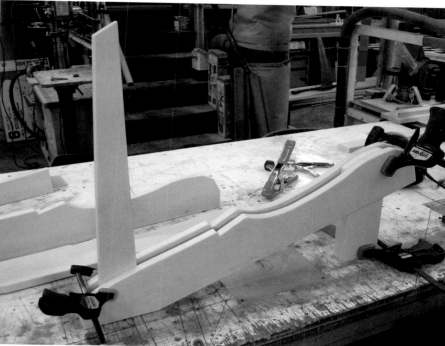

10 Be sure that the two center seat support pieces line up at the front or else the front seat slats will not rest evenly on both. Since you can't use the front locating blocks between the pieces, use a combination square across the front edges and clamp them together when they're even.

11 With the two center frame sections positioned and firmly clamped in place, fasten them together with carriage bolts.

Laying Out the Curves

To lay out the back support piece curves on the plywood pattern, first rip two 1/8" (3mm) strips of clear wood on the table saw. Working from the measurements on the scale/grid drawing, mark the two end points of the curve along the front edge of the pattern piece. Next mark the center point, set back the required distance from the edge. Using small nails in front of and behind the strip as shown in the photograph, set the strip in a fair curve that meets all three points, then mark it on the pattern piece. Once two equal curves are established using this method, the pattern piece is ready for cutting.

Using the measurements from the scale/grid drawing, make a plywood pattern to use as a shaping guide for each of the two back support frame pieces. Attach each pattern piece to a board with small brads or extra-strength, double-sided carpet tape. Cut to within an 1/8" (3mm) from the edge of the pattern with a jigsaw or band saw. After firmly clamping each piece to the work surface, trim away the excess material using a straight-cutting router bit with a pattern guide bearing. The back support pieces are now ready to install.

12 The upper and lower back supports connect the three seat-support assembly sections and provide support and attachment surfaces for the back slats. With the three seat-support frame sections equally spaced, attach the lower back support frame piece with silicone bronze screws.

13 Using bar clamps to hold it in place, predrill the first ipe seat slat and attach it to the seat support frame with silicone bronze screws.

14 Attach the first three seat slats against the flat cuts at the fronts of the seat support pieces and evenly distribute the rest along the curved surfaces. For now, install only the first four seat slats. This holds the front of the loveseat together but leaves plenty of working room to assemble the back.

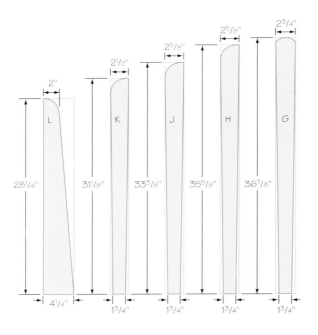

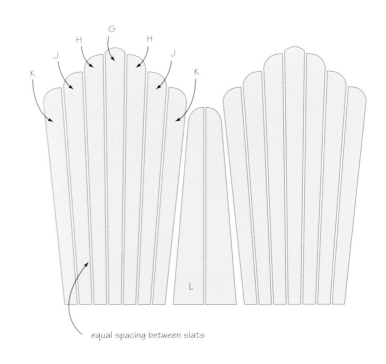

equal spacing between slats

Sizing the FanBack Slats

I like the fan-back look of the back slat layout, where the top of each slat is wider than the bottom. I used scraps and spacers along the upper and lower back support curves to calculate the individual slat measurements, experimenting with different slat and spacer dimensions until they came out right.

15 Using screws, attach the upper back support to the tops of the three vertical frame pieces. Use wood spacers and a strap clamp to make sure that the middle vertical frame piece is centered between the two outside vertical frame pieces during assembly. Once the upper back support is attached, lay the loveseat on its back. This will make it much easier to work on the back slats.

16 Using the dimensions calculated from laying out the back design, cut the tapered back slats, leaving them long at the top for the moment.

17 There's no magic to this layout. Use whatever shape looks good to mark out the curved back slat tops.

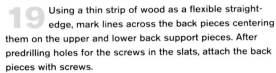

19 Using a thin strip of wood as a flexible straight-edge, mark lines across the back pieces centering them on the upper and lower back support pieces. After predrilling holes for the screws in the slats, attach the back pieces with screws.

18 With the back slats set in place on the back supports, use shims as spacers between the slats. Measure and cut the two back center spacers.

20 With the back completed, install the remaining seat slats. Be sure to double check the spacing between these slats.

TECHtip
avoid splitting
The arm supports are small and can easily split when the attachment screws are driven, especially when the top screw is driven through the arm into the ipe piece below. I had trouble with this so I used a metal tap to cut threads into the predrilled hardwood pieces.

21 Using the dimensions from the scale/grid drawings, make a plywood pattern for the arms. Make two arms using the same rough-cut-and-pattern-router method as you did with the seat support frame pieces. The arm supports are too small to safely use this method, so cut and shape them individually. Install the arms to the vertical frame pieces with screws in countersunk holes. Attach the arm supports to the arms by installing screws through the top of the arm and to the front vertical frame pieces with screws in countersunk holes. Plug all the screw holes.

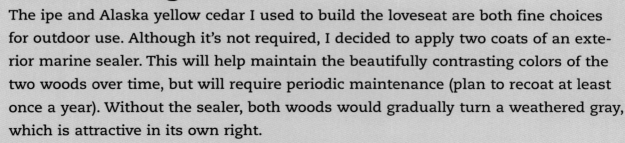

the finishing touch
The ipe and Alaska yellow cedar I used to build the loveseat are both fine choices for outdoor use. Although it's not required, I decided to apply two coats of an exterior marine sealer. This will help maintain the beautifully contrasting colors of the two woods over time, but will require periodic maintenance (plan to recoat at least once a year). Without the sealer, both woods would gradually turn a weathered gray, which is attractive in its own right.

bench seats and table

2

A *favorite landscape design feature* of my backyard is a small, compact deck. It's a great place to hang out with a beverage, but the low square footage is easily overwhelmed by a traditional garden table and four chairs. My solution to this problem was to develop a design for a small table and four bench seats that could be arranged in different seating configurations or moved out of the way completely if necessary. They also function nicely as side tables for lawn chairs and are sturdy enough to stand on to retrieve the cat from lower tree branches.

I chose to use teak for the tops and wenge for the frames and legs. The wenge was an experiment. It's a durable tropical hardwood and, when oiled, provides a striking contrast to the lighter teak.

I made all four benches as a single production run. This not only made the construction process faster and more efficient but also ensured that component sizing and dimensions were exactly the same for all of the benches. Although the measurements are different, I also made the table part of the production run, utilizing the same machine setups for the different steps.

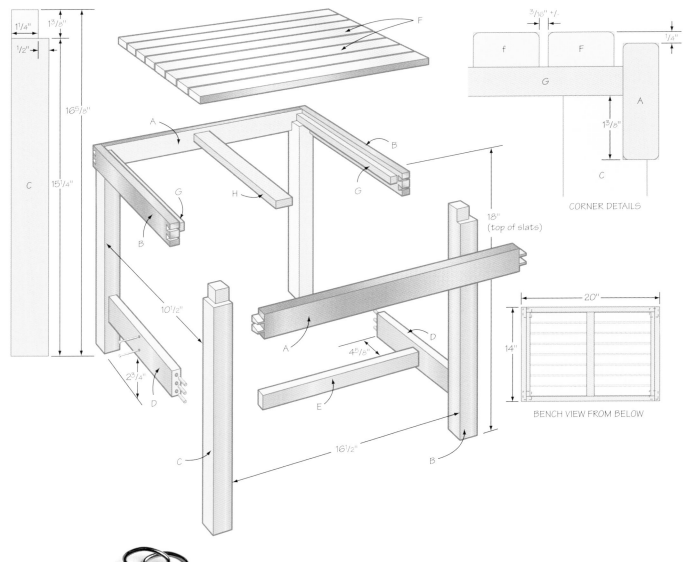

1¼" 1³⁄₈"

½"

16⁵⁄₈"

15¹⁄₄"

C

F

³⁄₁₆" +/-

¼"

f   F

G

A

1³⁄₈"

C

CORNER DETAILS

A

B

G

H

G

B

18"
(top of slats)

10¹⁄₂"

A

D

2³⁄₄"

D

45⁄₈"

E

C

B

16¹⁄₂"

20"

14"

BENCH VIEW FROM BELOW

hardware and supplies

³⁄₈" (10mm) × 2" (50mm) gluing dowels

1¹⁄₄" (30mm) stainless steel flathead screws

inches (millimeters)

REFERENCE	QUANTITY	PART	STOCK	THICKNESS	(mm)	WIDTH	(mm)	LENGTH	(mm)	COMMENTS
A	2	apron sides	wenge	3/4	(19)	2 1/2	(64)	20	(508)	
B	2	apron ends	wenge	3/4	(19)	2 1/2	(64)	14	(356)	
C	4	legs	wenge	1 3/4	(45)	1 3/4	(45)	16 5/8	(422)	
D	2	leg cross braces	wenge	3/4	(19)	2 1/2	(64)	10	(254)	
E	1	stretcher	wenge	3/4	(19)	2	(51)	15	(381)	
F	8	top slats	teak	3/4	(19)	1 3/8	(35)	18 1/8	(460)	3/16" +/- (5mm) between slats and between the slats, apron sides and ends
G	2	top slat cleats	wenge	5/8	(16)	3/4	(19)	12 1/2	(318)	
H	1	top slat center brace	teak	1 1/2	(38)	3/4	(19)	12 1/2	(318)	

TECHtip

Building furniture for outdoor use requires careful construction planning. Unlike the loveseat, which relies exclusively on mechanical fasteners, the bench seats are assembled using a combination of glued and mechanical joinery techniques. I was careful to choose a waterproof glue with some gap-filling capability and long-term flexibility and used outdoor-rated or SS screws. All countersunk screw holes that might collect water were glued and plugged.

1 Begin the bench by building the apron. Although a number of different joints could be used at the corners, I chose to use through dovetails. This provides a solid joint with lots of gluing surface and the interlocking design keeps the joint from separating or racking. I used a template jig system to machine-cut the dovetails. The only trick here was to be sure that the width dimension of the apron stock matched the jig's layout pattern. Measure the jig carefully and adjust the stock's width accordingly.

2 After applying glue to the dovetail pins and tails with a small brush, assemble the apron using bar clamps. Although the dovetail joints do a good preliminary job of squaring the assembly, carefully equalize opposing corner-to-corner measurements.

3 Much of the strength of the bench seat results from way that the legs are attached to the apron corners. Each leg has a shoulder cut into the tops of two adjacent sides and a corner of the apron rests on these shoulders. This design provides solid support for the apron-and-top assembly to supplement the mechanical fasteners. After cutting the legs to length, mark the faces to be cut with chalk. This helps keep track of the cutting sequence and prevents cutting errors.

TECH tip

dealing with router blowout

No matter how carefully I make router dovetail cuts in hardwoods, there is inevitably a chance for "blowout" or chipping when the bit catches the edge of the wood grain. I'm not a fan of putty or wood dough fillers because the color is never the same as the wood, even with stain and it doesn't hold up outdoors. I make my own filler using glue and sawdust from the wood I'm using. In this case I mixed wenge sawdust with a dark-colored waterproof glue.

4 After setting the blade height on the tablesaw, you're ready to make the first two shoulder cuts on each leg. Use the miter gauge and the starter block for safety.

5 Make the crosscuts on the two marked adjacent sides on each leg.

6 Finish the shoulder cuts on the band saw using a stop clamped to the table to limit the length of cut.

7 These legs are ready for assembly.

Miter Gauge Safety

To prevent stock from pinching against the fence and kicking back when you use the miter gauge, use a starter block. This is simply a scrap of wood clamped to the fence behind the leading edge of the blade. Adjust the fence so that the distance from the face of the block plus the blade kerf (in this case) equals the length of cut you need to make. With the stock held against the miter gauge, move it over to just touch the side of the block. Since the front edge of the block is behind the blade, the stock will be clear of both the fence and the block when the cut is made.

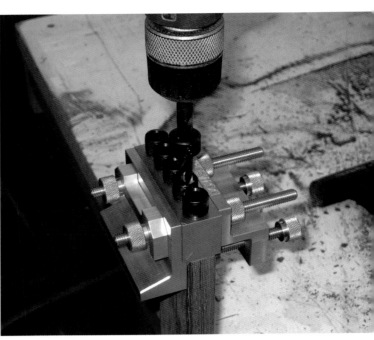

8 Now you're ready to assemble the two, leg-and-cross-brace assemblies using glue and dowels. First, put two legs in place on one end of the apron assembly. With the two legs firmly clamped in the apron end corners, take a measurement between the legs and cut the cross braces to length.

9 Use a doweling jig to drill holes for ³/₈" (10mm) dowels in the ends of the cross braces.

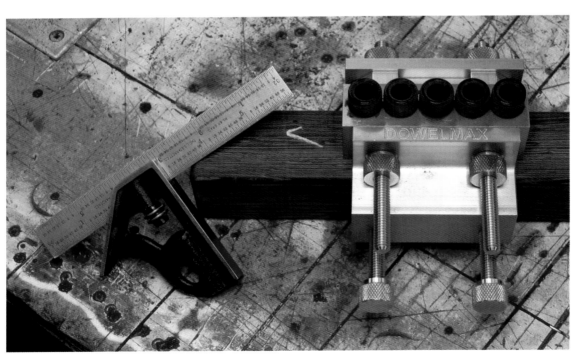

10 Drill holes in the legs to match the holes in the cross braces.

11 Using dowels and waterproof glue, assemble and clamp the leg-and-cross-brace assemblies.

12 Use a spacer cut to the same length as the cross brace so the legs will mate squarely to the brace.

13 The leg assemblies are now ready to be attached to the apron corners.

14 Cut spacers to fit snugly between the legs around all four sides of the inside of the apron. (These will hold the legs tightly in place against the corners during installation.) Apply glue to the two shoulder faces on each leg, set them into the corners and lock them snugly in place with the temporary spacers.

15 Attach each leg using two screws through the outside corners of the apron. Plug the screw holes. When the glue has dried, remove the temporary spacers.

16 After cutting the stretcher to length, position it between the leg cross braces, centering it on each cross brace using spacer blocks.

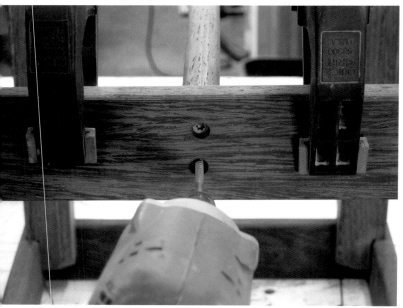

17 Install the stretcher using glue and countersunk screws. Plug the screw holes.

18 The top slats are supported by cleats at each end. Glue and screw the cleats to the insides of the end aprons and plug the screw holes.

19 Use spacers to hold equal spacing between the slats. Trim the spacers if necessary until the slats fit between the side aprons.

20 So no fasteners will show on the finished bench top, attach the slats from below. With the slats and spacers set loosely in place on the cleats, lay a piece of $^{1}/_{4}$" (6mm) plywood (slightly larger than the bench) over the top, then flip the entire assembly upside down on your work surface. If you're careful, the slats and spacers will all stay together inside the apron, ready for installation! Predrill into the slats through the cleats at each end and fasten the slats from below with screws. Attach a brace across the center of the slats from below with screws. Although probably not necessary, this brace adds stiffness and strength to the top slat assembly.

Build the Matching Table

The table closely follows the design of the bench seats. The material, joinery and construction sequences are exactly the same; only sizing and dimensions are different. The table is square and the top has a center hole for a patio umbrella. The design of the top slats, slat supports and stretchers have been modified to accommodate the umbrella and umbrella base, but those are the only structural differences.

inches (millimeters)

REFERENCE	QUANTITY	PART	STOCK	THICKNESS	(mm)	WIDTH	(mm)	LENGTH	(mm)	COMMENTS
SMALL TABLE										
J	4	apron sides	wenge	$^{3}/_{4}$	(19)	$2^{1}/_{2}$	(64)	25	(635)	
K	4	legs	wenge	$1^{3}/_{4}$	(45)	$1^{3}/_{4}$	(45)	$26^{5}/_{8}$	(676)	
L	2	leg cross braces	wenge	$^{3}/_{4}$	(19)	$2^{1}/_{2}$	(64)	21	(533)	
M	2	stretchers	wenge	$^{3}/_{4}$	(19)	2	(51)	22	(559)	
N	1	center top slat	teak	$^{3}/_{4}$	(19)	$3^{1}/_{2}$	(89)	$23^{1}/_{8}$	(587)	
P	8	top slats	teak	$^{3}/_{4}$	(19)	$2^{1}/_{8}$	(54)	$23^{1}/_{8}$	(587)	$^{3}/_{16}$" $^{+}/_{-}$ (5mm) between slats and between the slats, apron sides and ends
Q	2	top slat cleats	wenge	$^{5}/_{8}$	(16)	$^{3}/_{4}$	(19)	$23^{1}/_{2}$	(597)	
R	2	top slat center braces	teak	$1^{1}/_{2}$	(38)	$^{3}/_{4}$	(19)	$23^{1}/_{2}$	(597)	

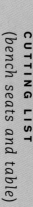

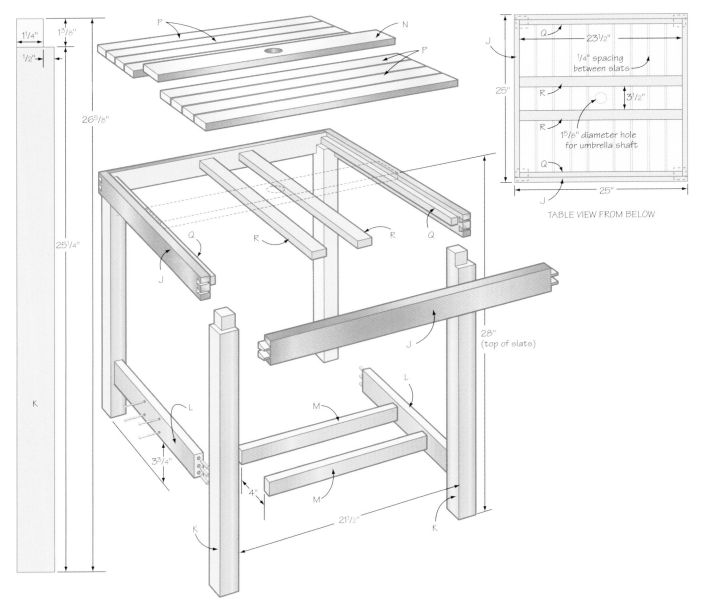

1¼"

1³/₈"

½"

26⁵/₈"

25¼"

K

P

N

P

Q

J

23½"

¼" spacing
between slats

25"

R

3½"

R

1⁵/₈" diameter hole
for umbrella shaft

Q

J

25"

TABLE VIEW FROM BELOW

J

Q

R

R

Q

J

J

28"
(top of slats)

J

L

L

M

M

3³/₄"

4"

K

K

21½"

hardware and supplies

³/₈" (10mm) × 2" (50mm) gluing dowels

1¼" (30mm) stainless steel flathead screws

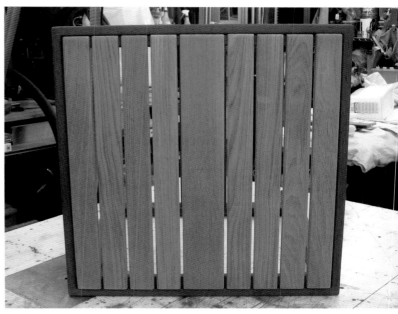

1 The bench seats have a single stretcher, but the table needs two — with enough space between them for the umbrella shaft and base. Using spacer blocks to hold the stretchers in position, attach the the stretcher with screws through the outside of the leg cross braces. Plug the screw holes.

2 The tabletop slats are proportionally wider than the bench seat slats. Make the center slat wider to accomodate the umbrella hole. Install two evenly-spaced teak braces below the slats for extra support.

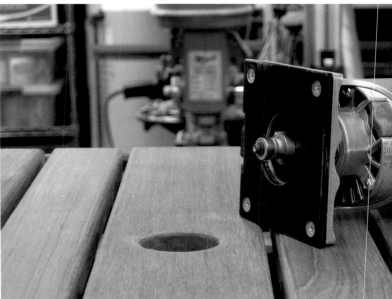

3 Drill a small pilot hole in the center of the tabletop. Then, using a sharp Forstner bit and drilling from both sides to avoid split-out, drill a $1^{5}/_{8}$" (40mm)-diameter hole through the slat.

4 Use a bearing-guided $^{1}/_{8}$" (3mm)-radius roundover bit and sandpaper to clean and finish the edges of the hole.

Apply Exterior Finish

As I said earlier, I like the contrast between the two woods I used for the benches and table. To protect against weathering and to keep the colors looking fresh, I applied a brush-on, wipe-off exterior oil sealer that I plan to reapply yearly.

garden fence with door

3

Into every life a little whimsy must fall and what better place for it to fall than into the garden? Some gardens feature fiberglass deer and ceramic bunnies, some have squads of gnomes lurking amid the shrubbery but, my garden has a door without a house. Not a ruin or a remnant of a former structure but an actual door surrounded by the great outdoors.

My wife and I came by it honestly— it was carefully planned. We knew that in one area of the garden we needed to hide an exposed section of house foundation. We considered plantings, rockery, camouflage netting — the works. In the end we settled on an architectural screen — a structure that exists only to hide or draw attention away from what's behind it.

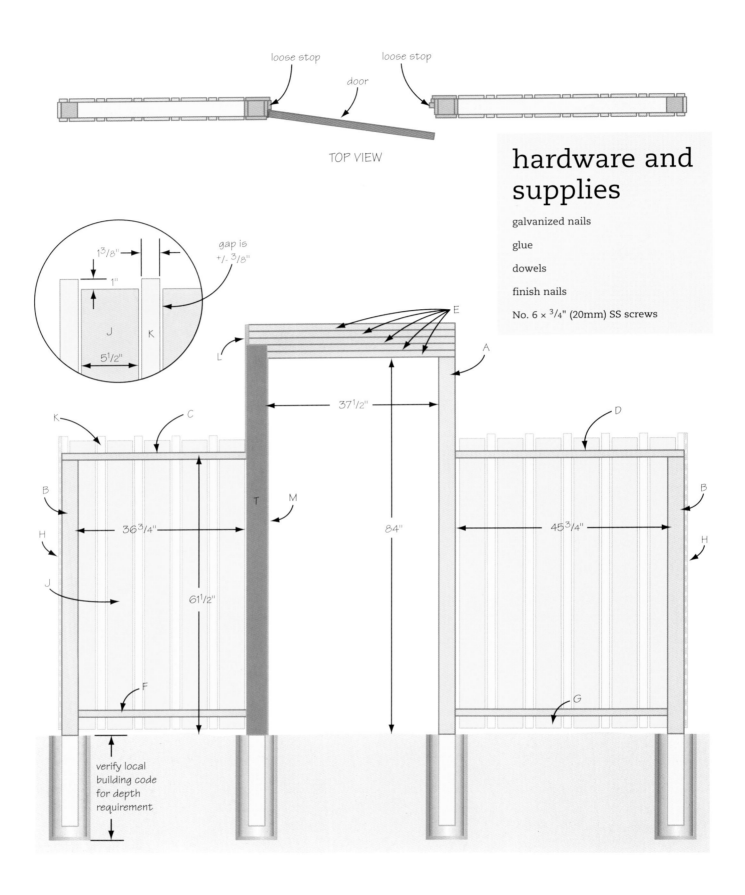

loose stop

loose stop

door

TOP VIEW

hardware and supplies

galvanized nails

glue

dowels

finish nails

No. 6 × 3/4" (20mm) SS screws

gap is +/- 3/8"

1 3/8"

1"

J

K

5 1/2"

E

L

A

K

C

D

37 1/2"

B

B

M

T

H

H

36 3/4"

45 3/4"

84"

J

61 1/2"

F

G

verify local building code for depth requirement

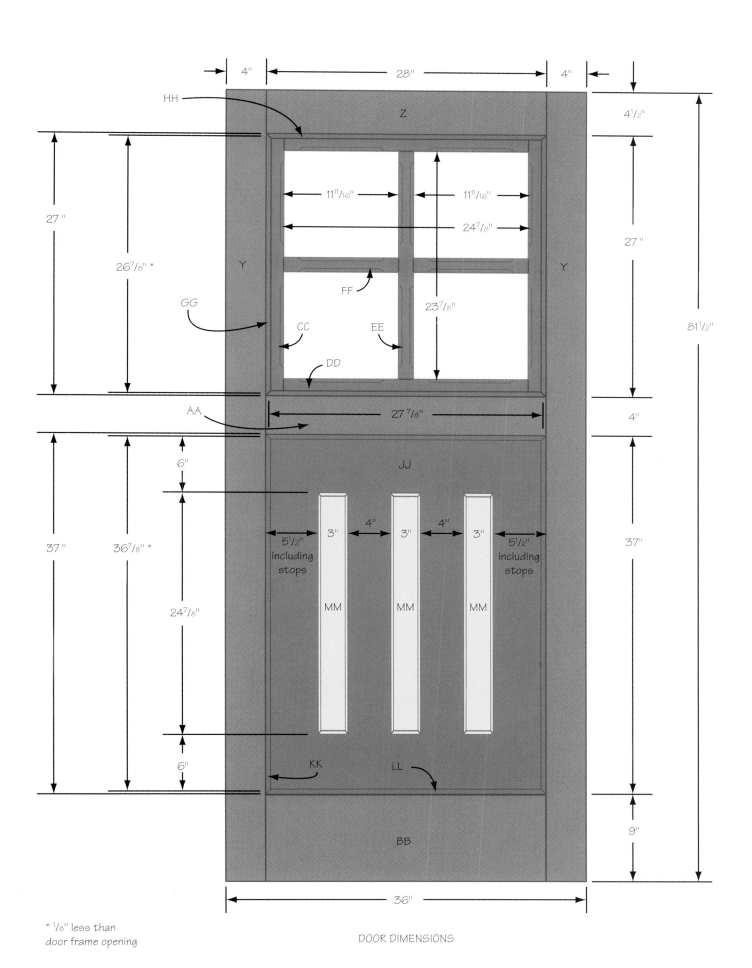

4"   28"   4"

HH

Z

4¹/₂"

27"

26⁷/₈" *

Y   11¹¹/₁₆"   11¹¹/₁₆"   Y   27"

24⁷/₈"

GG   FF

23⁷/₈"

CC   EE

DD

81¹/₂"

AA   27 ⁷/₈"

4"

6"   JJ

37"   36⁷/₈" *

4"   4"   37"

5¹/₂"
including
stops   3"   3"   3"   5¹/₂"
including
stops

24⁷/₈"

MM   MM   MM

6"

KK   LL

9"

BB

36"

* ¹/₈" less than
door frame opening

DOOR DIMENSIONS

inches (millimeters)

REFERENCE	QUANTITY	PART	STOCK	THICKNESS	(mm)	WIDTH	(mm)	LENGTH	(mm)	COMMENTS
FENCE AND DOOR OPENING										
A	2	door frame posts		$3^1/_2$	(89)	$3^1/_2$	(89)	84	(2134)	leave long, set in concrete, then cut to final length in place
B	2	fence end posts		$3^1/_2$	(89)	$3^1/_2$	(89)	$61^1/_2$	(1562)	leave long, set in concrete, then cut to final length in place
C	1	short side top rail		$1^1/_2$	(38)	$3^1/_2$	(89)	$40^1/_4$	(1022)	
D	1	long side top rail		$1^1/_2$	(38)	$3^1/_2$	(89)	$49^1/_4$	(1251)	
E	5	door frame top rails		$1^1/_2$	(38)	$3^1/_2$	(89)	$44^1/_2$	(1131)	
F	1	short side bottom rail		$1^1/_2$	(38)	$3^1/_2$	(89)	$36^3/_4$	(933)	
G	1	long side bottom rail		$1^1/_2$	(38)	$3^1/_2$	(89)	$45^3/_4$	(1162)	
H	2	end post sheath board	cedar	$3/_4$	(19)	$3^1/_2$	(89)	65	(1651)	top to be 2" (51mm) above top rail
J	22	wide fence boards	cedar	$3/_4$	(19)	$5^1/_2$	(140)	65	(1651)	top to be 2" (51mm) above top rail
K	22	narrow fence boards	cedar	$3/_4$	(19)	$1^3/_4$	(45)	66	(1676)	top to be 3" (76mm) above top rail
L	2	post outer side sheath boards	cedar	$3/_4$	(19)	$3^1/_2$	(89)	$25^3/_8$	(724)	paint #1 (dark blue), attach to post outer side above fence top rail
M	2	post inner side sheath boards	cedar	$3/_4$	(19)	$3^1/_2$	(89)	84	(2134)	paint #1 (dark blue)
N	1	frame header inner side sheath board	cedar	$3/_4$	(19)	$3^1/_2$	(89)	$35^1/_4$	(895)	paint #1 (dark blue)
P	1	hinge side loose stop	cedar	$3/_4$	(19)	2	(51)	$83^1/_4$	(2114)	paint #1 (dark blue)
Q	1	strike side loose stop backer	cedar	$3/_4$	(19)	$1^1/_8$	(22)	$83^1/_4$	(2114)	paint #1 (dark blue)
R	1	strike side loose stop	Douglas fir	$1^1/_8$	(29)	$7/_8$	(29)	$83^1/_4$	(2114)	paint #1 (dark blue)
S	2	post rear face sheath boards	cedar	$3/_4$	(19)	$5^1/_4$	(133)	87	(2210)	paint #1 (dark blue)
T	2	post front face sheath boards	cedar	$3/_4$	(19)	$4^1/_2$	(115)	87	(2210)	paint #1 (dark blue)
U	2	door frame top rail sheath boards	cedar	$3/_4$	(19)	$3^1/_2$	(89)	37	(940)	paint #1 (dark blue)
V	2	top middle casing trim boards	Douglas fir	1	(25)	$3^3/_4$	(95)	$51^1/_2$	(1308)	paint #2 (light blue)
W	2	top upper casing trim boards	Douglas fir	$1^1/_4$	(32)	$2^3/_4$	(70)	$57^1/_2$	(1461)	paint #3 (hunter green)
X	1	top trim cap board	Douglas fir	$3/_4$	(19)	$6^1/_2$	(165)	58	(1473)	paint #3 (hunter green)
NN	2	middle casing trim ends	Douglas fir	$3/_4$	(19)	$3^5/_8$	(92)	$6^1/$	(165)	paint #2 (light blue)
PP	2	top casing trim ends	Douglas fir	$3/_4$	(19)	$3^5/_8$	(92)	$2^3/_4$	(70)	paint #3 (hunter green)
DOOR										
Y	2	stiles	cedar	$1^1/_2$	(38)	4	(102)	$81^1/_2$	(2070)	paint #5 (purple)
Z	1	top rail	cedar	$1^1/_2$	(38)	5	(127)	28	(711)	paint #5 (purple)
AA	1	intermediate (lock) rail	cedar	$1^1/_2$	(38)	4	(102)	28	(711)	paint #5 (purple)
BB	1	bottom rail	cedar	$1^1/_2$	(38)	9	(229)	28	(711)	paint #5 (purple)
CC	2	outside stiles	Douglas fir	$3/_4$	(19)	$1^1/_2$	(38)	$26^7/_8$	(682)	paint #5 (purple), rout stopped cove detail around inside opening
DD	2	top/bottom rails	Douglas fir	$3/_4$	(19)	$1^1/_2$	(38)	$24^7/_8$	(632)	paint #5 (purple), rout stopped cove detail around inside opening
EE	1	center stile	Douglas fir	$3/_4$	(19)	$1^1/_2$	(38)	$23^7/_8$	(606)	paint #5 (purple), rout stopped cove detail around inside opening
FF	2	center rails	Douglas fir	$3/_4$	(19)	$1^1/_2$	(38)	$11^{11}/_{16}$	(297)	paint #5 (purple), rout stopped cove detail around inside opening
GG	4	vertical stops	quarter round	$7/_{16}$	(6)	$7/_{16}$	(11)	27	(686)	paint #5 (purple)
HH	4	horizontal stops	quarter round	$7/_{16}$	(6)	$7/_{16}$	(11)	28	(711)	paint #5 (purple)
JJ	1	panel	plywood	$1/_2$	(13)	$27^7/_8$	(708)	$36^7/_8$	(936)	paint #6 (yellow), marine plywood
KK	4	vertical stops	quarter round	$7/_{16}$	(11)	$7/_{16}$	(11)	37	(940)	paint #6 (yellow)
LL	4	horizontal stops	quarter round	$7/_{16}$	(11)	$7/_{16}$	(11)	28	(711)	paint #6 (yellow)
MM	6	applied accent piece	Douglas fir	$3/_4$	(19)	4	(102)	$24^7/_8$	(632)	rout cove detail around outside edges, attach 3 to each side of the plywood panel

Planning and Layout

After considering various options we decided to install a free-standing section of cedar fencing identical to the fencing that encloses our backyard. This might sound a bit boring, but we threw in a twist that made all the difference. I decided to make one section of the fence into an entry to the garden beyond, but instead of a traditional gate we opted to install a residential exterior-style door. And not just any old door, but a door and door frame painted in multiple bright colors. First — only for interest — I set the length of fence at a slight angle to the existing adjacent concrete walkway. The fence posts and the posts that frame the door opening are traditional 4×4 ground-contact treated Douglas fir and the door opening has a framed header for additional support. The door frame sheathing and jamb stock are painted. The fence boards are alternating 1×6 and 1×2 tight-knot rough cedar.

A Plan for Power

Since things were going to be dug up anyway, I took the opportunity to dig a trench through the lower garden and bring in an underground electrical line. This allowed me to plan for electrical power at the BBQ station and the tool shed and also to install an outdoor electrical outlet at one end of the fence.

1 Following the provisions of the local electrical code, I dug a trench and installed special underground wire, conduit and boxes.

2 I covered the wire in the trench with treated 2x material as additional protection against potential damage from future digging.

Power Up – But Do It Right

Having access to electricity in the garden is great, but outdoor wiring requires special procedures and components. Get an electrical permit, follow all appropriate electrical code provisions and have the project inspected as required. Remember: water and electricity don't mix!

Build the Fence and Doorway Support Frame

Build the fence and doorway support structure just like you would for a fence. Use ground contact treated 4×4s set in concrete for the posts, and above-ground treated 2×4s for the rails.

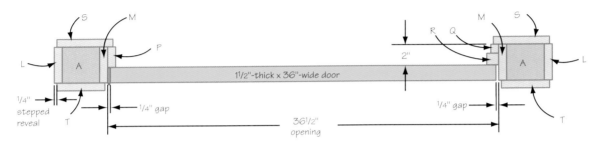

DOOR FRAME SIDES AND TRIM - TOP VIEW

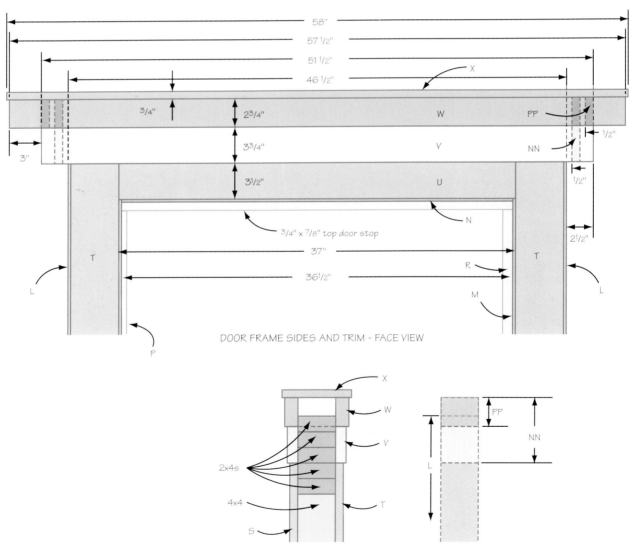

DOOR FRAME SIDES AND TRIM - FACE VIEW

DOOR FRAME SIDES AND TRIM - SIDE VIEW

3 I planned to use a standard 82" × 36" (200 × 90) door, so I sized the opening accordingly. The door opening is higher than the top of the fence and I installed a structural header assembly for strength.

4 Install an extra treated 2×6 rail to support the outdoor electrical outlet box.

5 Using galvanized nails, install the painted jamb stock and post wrap trim pieces first. Prime and paint all the pieces in the shop before installation.

7 With the doorway trim in place, install the fence boards. The first step is to check your layout and measurements. Know the widths of the two sizes of fence boards you're using and the approximate gap that you want between them. Begin the installation by attaching a 1×4 fence board to the end face of one 4×4 end post. Set it to the height above the top rail for the 1×6 fence boards, then run a string line at that height to the sheathed 4×4 door frame post.

6 Install the painted trim pieces above the door opening to cover the header structure.

8 You now know the exact distance you need between the 1×6 fence boards. To make the installation easier, make a spacer jig to precisely position the boards before nailing. This eliminates the need to measure each gap to achieve uniformity and accuracy.

9 Attach 1×6 fence boards to the string height using the spacer jig.

10 Set a new string line and attach the 1×2 fence boards to this new height, centering them in the gaps between the 1×6's.

11 The alternating wide and narrow boards provide a nice visual rhythm.

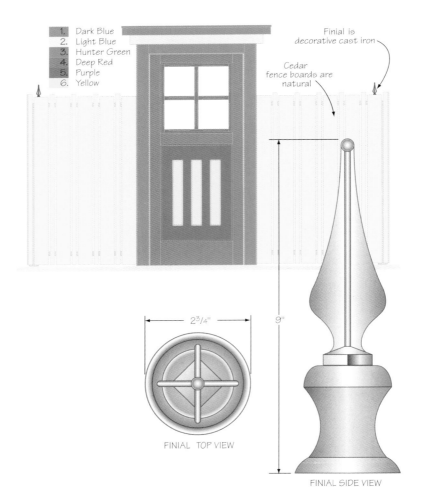

1. Dark Blue
2. Light Blue
3. Hunter Green
4. Deep Red
5. Purple
6. Yellow

Finial is decorative cast iron

Cedar fence boards are natural

2³/₄"

9"

FINIAL TOP VIEW

FINIAL SIDE VIEW

12 Although I could have used a house door from a salvage yard, I chose to make my own. The door is completely exposed to the weather and the elements and I was worried that a standard door — even an exterior door — would not hold together over time. I used 2× kiln-dried clear cedar for the frame because of its light weight and good outdoor survival characteristics. Drill double dowel holes in the stiles and rails of the door-frame parts.

13 Assemble the door frame using waterproof glue and dowels.

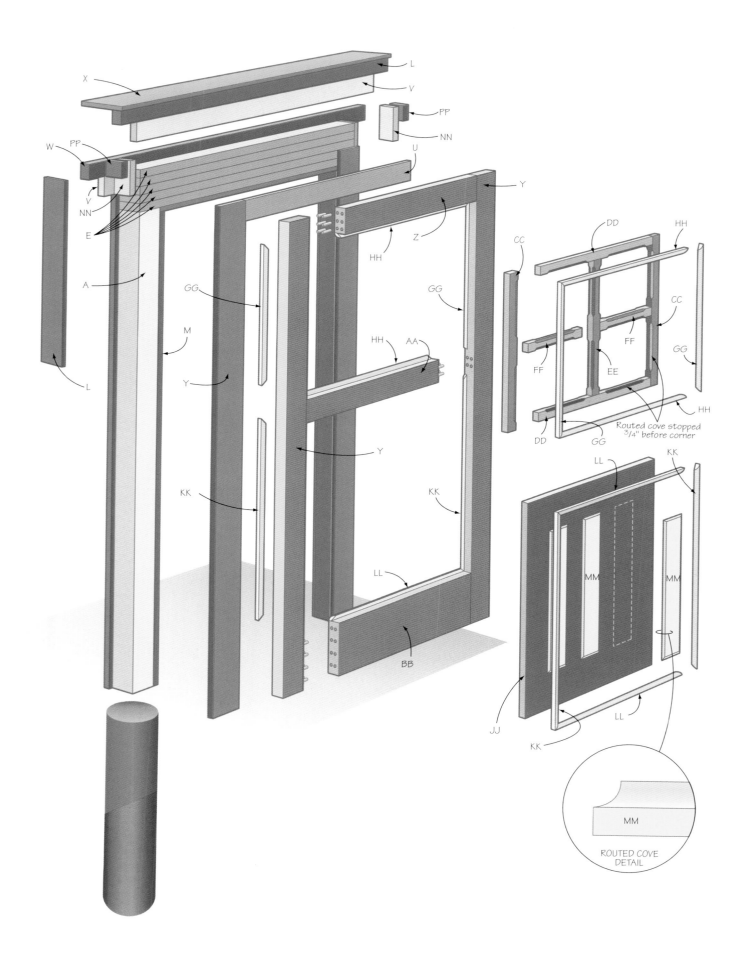

Routed cove stopped
3/4" before corner

ROUTED COVE
DETAIL

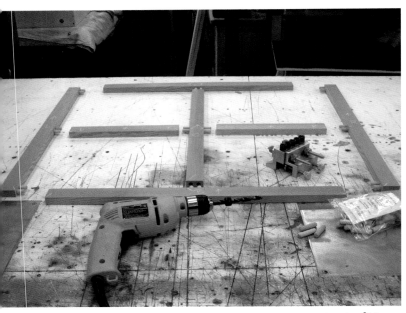

14 I built the upper crosspiece panel from Douglas fir using $^3/_8$" (10mm) gluing dowels and waterproof glue. Prime it with bleed-proof primer before painting.

15 After painting the upper cross piece panel, predrill and install it using galvanized finish nails. Then, install the $^1/_4$" (6mm) quarter-round stops.

16 Build the lower panel and detail pieces. I primed and painted all the pieces before final assembly. Then, attach the yellow detail pieces directly on the panel using No. 6 stainless-steel screws. Hold the panel in place with the $^7/_{16}$" (11mm) quarter-round stops.

18 For a crowning touch, I installed decorative finials on the tops of the two fence ends. I used cast iron hose guides and set them on blocks using polyurethane glue, which expands as it dries. This holds the finials in place. Finish the fence with an outdoor oil sealer to protect it from the elements.

17 I used standard door hinges and an ornamental exterior latchset. I wanted to keep it simple and functional. Since the installation is outdoors, there is potential for more wood movement and swelling than is normal for a standard house door. To compensate for this, I left a $^3/_8$" (10mm) reveal along the sides of the door, which is a little more than the usual $^1/_4$" (6mm) reveal.

potting bench

4

Behind every serious gardener there's usually a serious potting bench. This outdoor work station sees year-round use — from starting seeds in the spring, to repotting and through fall and winter cleanup. Potting benches are sometimes available at garden centers and through specialty catalogs, but my impression is that they're usually pretty light-duty. The design I've developed is more industrial-strength than boutique but it has a bit of style thrown in for good measure.

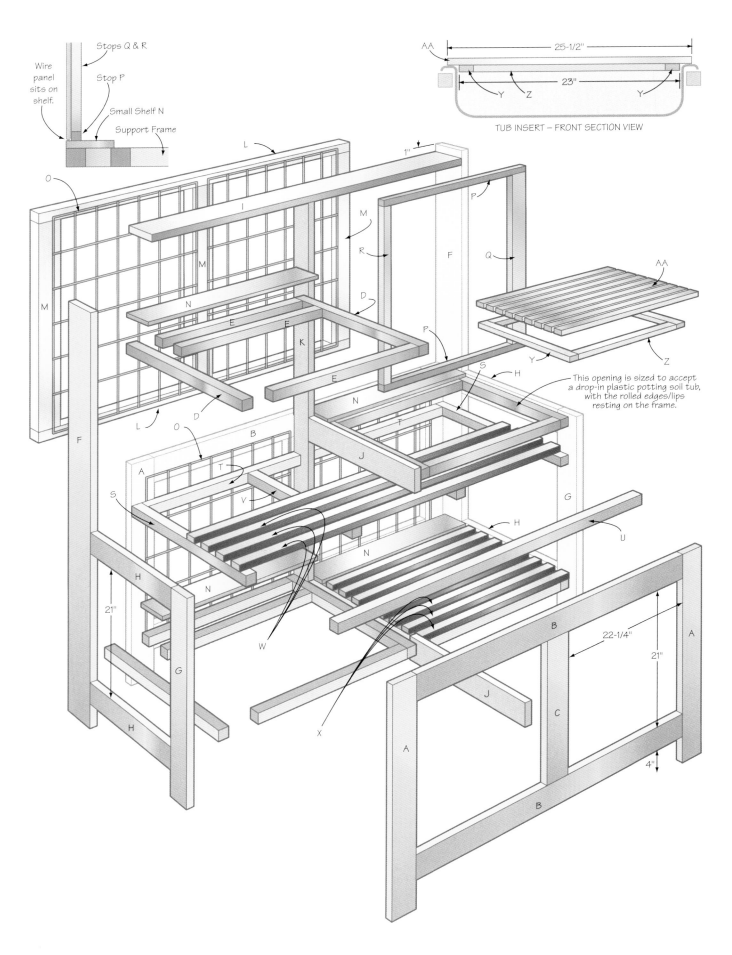

Wire panel sits on shelf.

Stops Q & R

Stop P

Small Shelf N

Support Frame

TUB INSERT – FRONT SECTION VIEW

25-1/2"

23"

AA

Y   Z   Y

This opening is sized to accept a drop-in plastic potting soil tub, with the rolled edges/lips resting on the frame.

1"

21"

22-1/4"

21"

4"

inches (millimeters)

REFERENCE	QUANTITY	PART	STOCK	THICKNESS	(mm)	WIDTH	(mm)	LENGTH	(mm)	COMMENTS
A	4	outside stiles	5/4×4 cedar	1	(25)	$3^1/2$	(89)	32	(813)	
B	4	top & bottom rails	5/4×4 cedar	1	(25)	$3^1/2$	(89)	48	(1219)	
C	2	center stiles	5/4×4 edar	1	(25)	$3^1/2$	(89)	21	(533)	
D	8	outside frame pieces	2×2 cedar	$1^1/2$	(25)	$1^1/2$	(25)	25	(635)	
E	12	inside frame pieces	2×2 cedar	$1^1/2$	(25)	$1^1/2$	(25)	24	(610)	
F	2	back vertical frame pieces	5/4×6 cedar	1	(25)	$5^1/2$	(140)	68	(1727)	
G	2	front vertical frame pieces	5/4×4 cedar	1	(25)	$3^1/2$	(89)	32	(813)	
H	4	side horiz. frame pieces	5/4×4 cedar	1	(25)	$3^1/2$	(89)	19	(483)	
I	1	top shelf	5/4×6 cedar	1	(25)	$5^1/2$	(140)	55	(1397)	
J	1	lower horiz. frame piece	5/4×4 cedar	1	(25)	$3^1/2$	(89)	$21^1/2$	(546)	
K	2	back cntr vert frame piece	5/4×4 cedar	1	(25)	$3^1/2$	(89)	$58^1/2$	(1486)	
L	2	top & bottom rails	5/4×2 cedar	1	(25)	$1^1/2$	(38)	55	(1397)	
M	3	stiles	5/4×4 cedar	1	(25)	$3^1/2$	(89)	31	(787)	
N	4	small back shelves	5/4×6 cedar	1	(25)	$4^3/8$	(111)	27	(686)	
O	4	wire mesh panels	steel*	N/A		N/A		*		galvanized steel wire fence 4" (102mm), cut to fit
P	8	horizontal stops	5/4×5/4 cedar	1	(25)	1	(25)	27	(686)	
Q	4	outside vertical stops	5/4×3 cedar	1	(25)	$2^1/2$	(64)	CTF		cut to fit
R	4	inside vertical stops	5/4×5/4 cedar	1	(25)	1	(25)	CTF		cut to fit
S	2	side frame pieces	2×2 cedar	$1^1/2$	(25)	$1^1/2$	(25)	25	(635)	
T	2	back frame pieces	2×2 cedar	$1^1/2$	(25)	$1^1/2$	(25)	$25^1/2$	(648)	
U	1	front frame piece	2×2 cedar	$1^1/2$	(25)	$1^1/2$	(25)	55	(1397)	
V	2	intermediate frame pieces	2×2 cedar	$1^1/2$	(25)	$1^1/2$	(25)	22	(559)	
W	8	upper shelf slats	1×2 cedar	$3/4$	(19)	$1^1/2$	(25)	55	(1397)	
X	20	lower shelf slats	1×2 cedar	$3/4$	(19)	$1^1/2$	(25)	$26^3/4$	(679)	
Y	4	frame stiles	1×2 cedar	$3/4$	(19)	$1^1/2$	(25)	17	(432)	
Z	4	frame rails	1×2 cedar	$3/4$	(19)	$1^1/2$	(25)	20	(508)	
AA	18	tub cover slats	1×2 cedar	$3/4$	(19)	$1^1/2$	(25)	$25^1/2$	(648)	
BB	1	upper horiz. frame piece	5/4×4 cedar	1	(25)	$3^1/2$	(89)	25	(635)	

hardware and supplies

No. 8 × $1^1/4$" (30mm) outdoor-rated pocket-hole screws

No. 8 × 2" (50mm) deck screws

No. 8 × 2" (50mm) outdoor-rated washer-head screws

Planning and Layout

The starting point for my design was the work top. I wanted a traditional slat surface, but I also wanted tub containers that could hold potting soil. In the end I combined these design elements into two framed openings that could accept either a slat insert or a plastic tub. I found a plastic tub I liked at a farm supply store and adjusted the construction dimensions to its measurements, but it would be easy to change the layout to fit another tub size.

I chose to use dimensional lumber whenever possible to keep costs down, and also to make construction easier. The main frame components are made from 5/4 tight-knot (TK) cedar decking, which comes with all four edges rounded over. The tub/slat insert support frames are made from 2×2 clear cedar, and the slats are 1×2 clear cedar. All screws and fasteners are outdoor/deck-rated. There's no fancy joinery or glue joints in the construction — just a straight-ahead, no-frills design.

1 Using outdoor-rated pocket-hole screws, assemble the identical front and lower back face frames ABC.

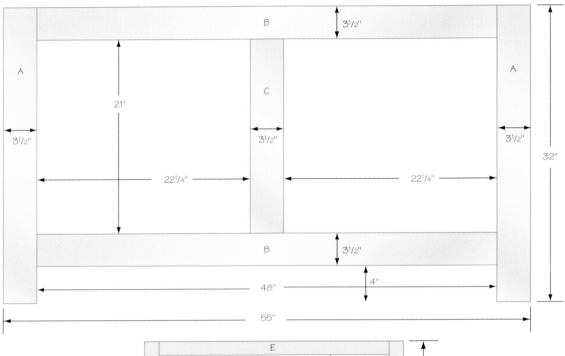

2 Using 2×2 cedar and 2" (50mm) deck screws, begin by building four identical support frames DE: two for the top surface to house the tubs or slat inserts, and two more for the bottom slat shelves.

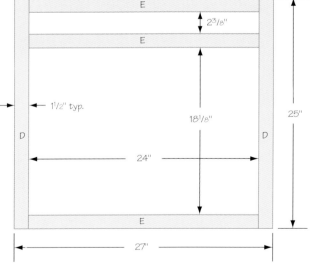

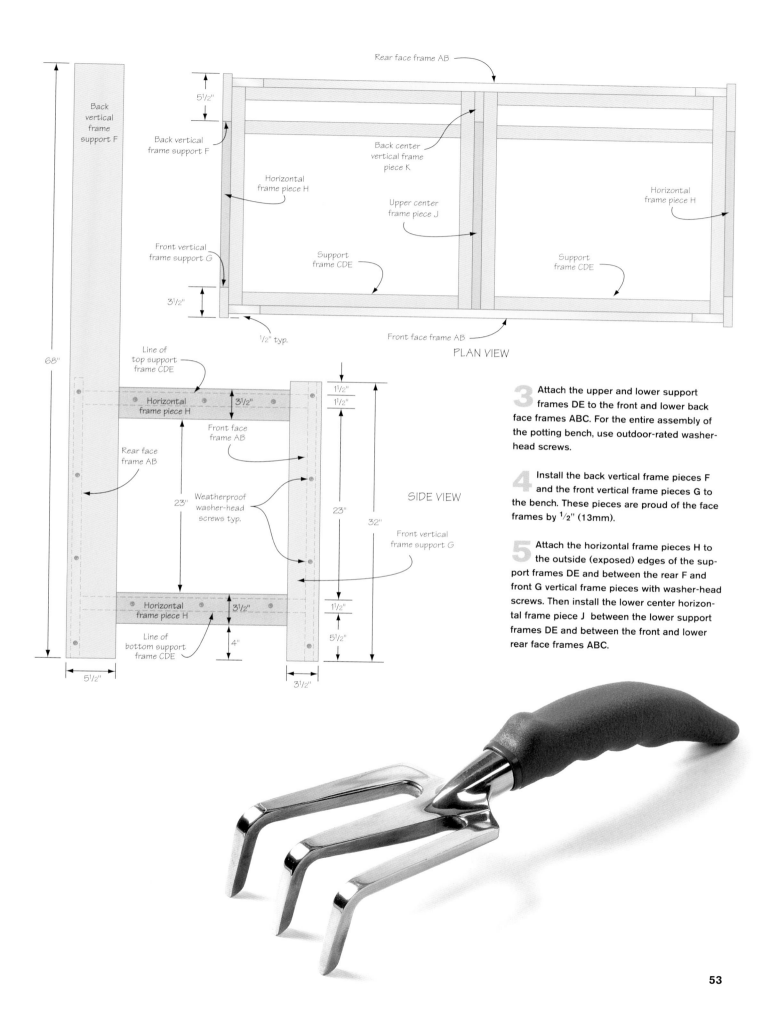

Rear face frame AB

Back vertical frame support F

Back vertical frame support F

5¹/₂"

Back center vertical frame piece K

Horizontal frame piece H

Horizontal frame piece H

Upper center frame piece J

Front vertical frame support G

3¹/₂"

Support frame CDE

Support frame CDE

68"

¹/₂" typ.

Front face frame AB

PLAN VIEW

Line of top support frame CDE

1¹/₂"

1¹/₂"

Horizontal frame piece H

3¹/₂"

Front face frame AB

Rear face frame AB

23"

Weatherproof washer-head screws typ.

23"

32"

SIDE VIEW

Front vertical frame support G

Horizontal frame piece H

3¹/₂"

1¹/₂"

Line of bottom support frame CDE

4"

5¹/₂"

5¹/₂"

3¹/₂"

3 Attach the upper and lower support frames DE to the front and lower back face frames ABC. For the entire assembly of the potting bench, use outdoor-rated washer-head screws.

4 Install the back vertical frame pieces F and the front vertical frame pieces G to the bench. These pieces are proud of the face frames by ¹/₂" (13mm).

5 Attach the horizontal frame pieces H to the outside (exposed) edges of the support frames DE and between the rear F and front G vertical frame pieces with washer-head screws. Then install the lower center horizontal frame piece J between the lower support frames DE and between the front and lower rear face frames ABC.

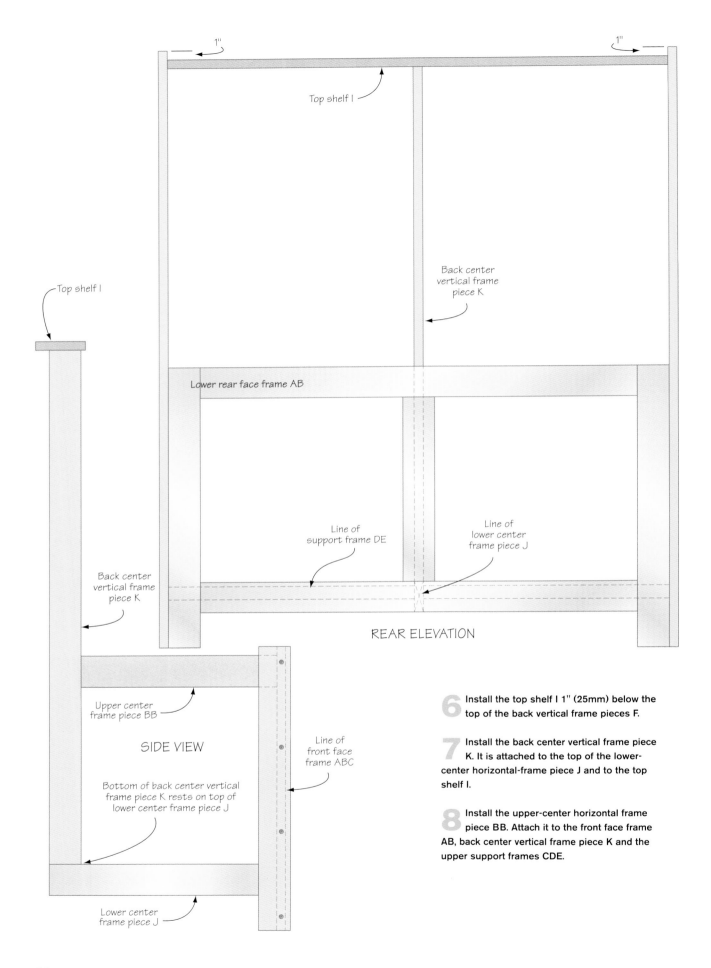

1"

1"

Top shelf I

Back center
vertical frame
piece K

Top shelf I

Lower rear face frame AB

Line of
support frame DE

Line of
lower center
frame piece J

Back center
vertical frame
piece K

REAR ELEVATION

Upper center
frame piece BB

SIDE VIEW

Line of
front face
frame ABC

Bottom of back center vertical
frame piece K rests on top of
lower center frame piece J

Lower center
frame piece J

6 Install the top shelf I 1" (25mm) below the top of the back vertical frame pieces F.

7 Install the back center vertical frame piece K. It is attached to the top of the lower-center horizontal-frame piece J and to the top shelf I.

8 Install the upper-center horizontal frame piece BB. Attach it to the front face frame AB, back center vertical frame piece K and the upper support frames CDE.

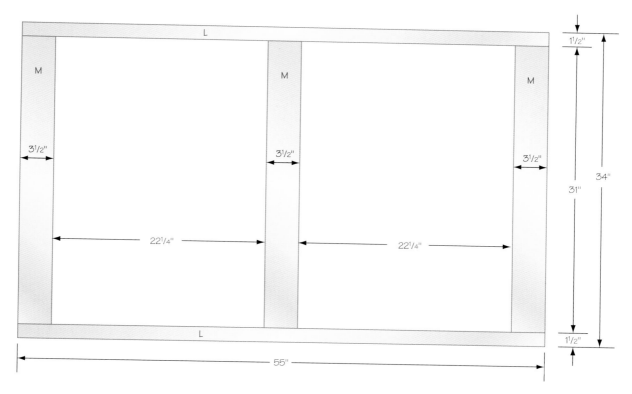

9 Attach the upper rear face-frame parts in place.

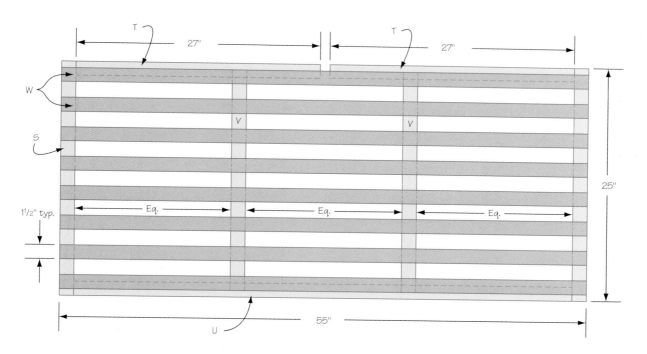

10 Assemble the upper slat shelf STUVW. This shelf supports the bottoms of the tubs.

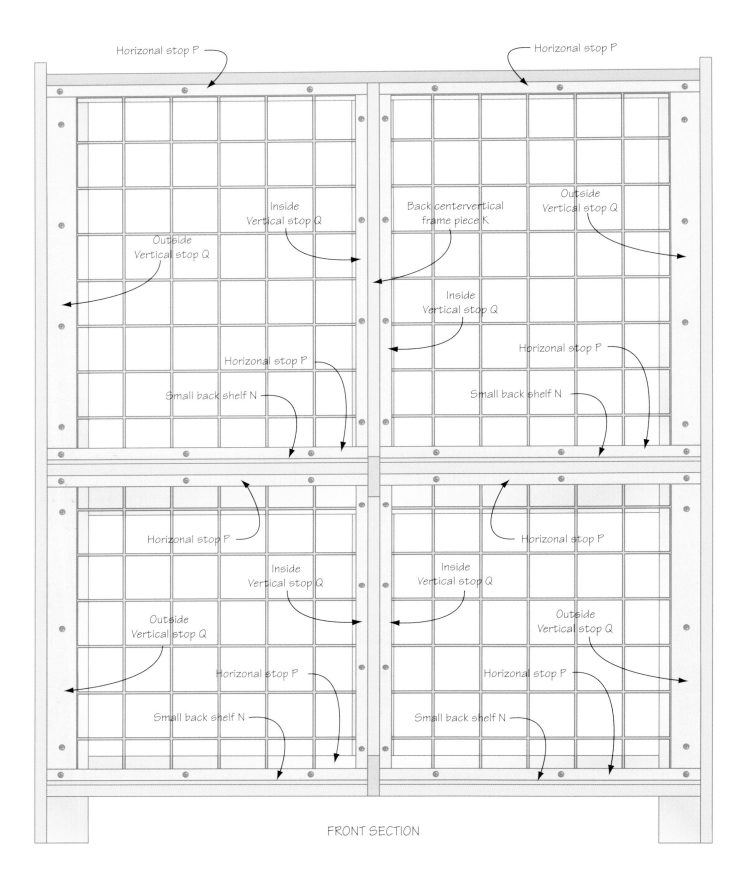

Horizonal stop P

Horizonal stop P

Inside
Vertical stop Q

Back centervertical
frame piece K

Outside
Vertical stop Q

Outside
Vertical stop Q

Inside
Vertical stop Q

Horizonal stop P

Horizonal stop P

Small back shelf N

Small back shelf N

Horizonal stop P

Horizonal stop P

Inside
Vertical stop Q

Inside
Vertical stop Q

Outside
Vertical stop Q

Outside
Vertical stop Q

Horizonal stop P

Horizonal stop P

Small back shelf N

Small back shelf N

FRONT SECTION

11 Cut the upper and lower back galvanized fence grids to size with bolt cutters
and install them using wood stops against the upper and lower back face
frames. I chose this grid material because it's completely weatherproof, is open, lets
light through and makes a great place to hang tools, watering cans and so forth.

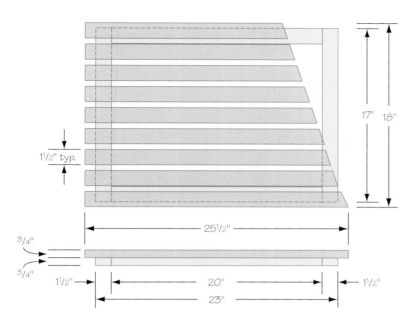

17" 18"

1½" typ.

25½"

¾"

¾"

1½" 20" 1½"

23"

12 Assemble the tubs inserts. These inserts provide a work surface that will let potting soil or whatever fall between the slats and land in the tub below.

13 I didn't apply any finish or sealer to the potting bench. I chose to let the cedar naturally turn to a weathered gray color. I did, however, soak the bottoms of the corner frame pieces in sealer where they rest on the ground.

covered
BBQ station

I would like to state, for the record, that I am not a barbecue fanatic! Although I admire and respect those people who devote their leisure time to filling the neighborhood with clouds of aromatic smoke, I personally make an attempt to cultivate other interests and lead a well-rounded life.

I do, however, admit to more than a passing interest in barbecuing. I have, on occasion, been spotted huddled next to a covered grill during a snowstorm. My family accepts that I routinely venture out into the dark of night and pouring rain to barbecue with the aid of an umbrella and a headlamp. Recognizing that these behaviors probably will not change, I decided that it would make good sense to build a covered BBQ station.

5

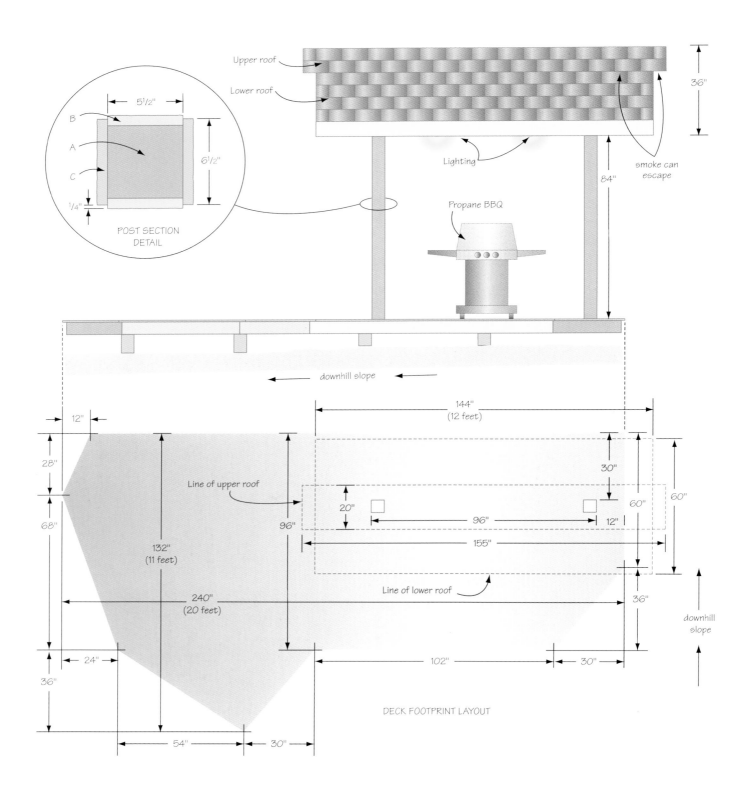

5¹/₂"

B

A

6¹/₂"

C

¹/₄"

POST SECTION
DETAIL

Upper roof

Lower roof

36"

Lighting

smoke can
escape

Propane BBQ

84"

downhill slope

144"
(12 feet)

12"

28"

Line of upper roof

30"

20"

60"

60"

68"

96"

96"

12"

155"

132"
(11 feet)

Line of lower roof

240"
(20 feet)

36"

24"

downhill
slope

36"

102"

30"

DECK FOOTPRINT LAYOUT

54"

30"

inches (millimeters)

REFERENCE	QUANTITY	PART	STOCK	THICKNESS	(mm)	WIDTH	(mm)	LENGTH	(mm)	COMMENTS
ROOF STRUCTURE										
A	2	posts/uprights	6×6 treated	5½	(140)	5½	(140)	14'	(4.66m)	verify length, check codes for correct depth in ground
B	4	narrow sheath boards	1×6 cedar	¾	(19)	3½	(89)	10'	(3.04m)	rough side out, cut to length
C	4	wide sheath boards	1×6 cedar	¾	(19)	4½	(114)	10'	(3.04m)	rough side out, cut to length
D	2	ridge boards	2×6 fir	1½	(38)	5½	(140)	12'	(3.66m)	double ridge of lower roof, sandwiches post
E	2	lower roof frame fascia	2×6 fir	1½	(38)	5½	(140)	12'	(3.66m)	cut to length
F	14	lower-roof rafters	2×6 fir	1½	(38)	5½	(140)	40	(145)	cut to length and angle
G	8	rafter cross ties	2×6 fir	1½	(38)	5½	(140)	65	(864)	cut to length and angle
H	8	upper-roof supports	2×6 fir	1½	(38)	5½	(140)	28	(711)	cut to length and angle
I	*	lower-roof skip sheathing	2×6 fir	¾	(19)	3½	(89)	12'	(3.66m)	*quantity as needed
J	2	upper-roof decks	1×12 cedar	¾	(19)	11¼	(286)	14'	(4.25m)	rip one edge to match roof angle
K	*	roof material of choice	cedar	N/A		N/A		N/A		*verify number of courses and exposure area
JOIST FOUNDATION SUPPORTS										
L	1	short beam	4×6 treated	3½	(140)	5½	(89)	8'	(2.5m)	2 galvanized metal saddle anchors set in concrete
M	1	long beam	4×6 treated	3½	(89)	5½	(89)	10'	(3m)	3 galvanized metal saddle anchors set in concrete
N	3	short beams	4×4 treated	3½	(89)	3½	(89)	8'	(2.5m)	set on concrete blocks
DECK JOIST FRAMING										
O	8	Long framers	2×6 fir	1½	(38)	5½	(140)	20'	(6m)	cut to length and angle
P	1	short framer	2×6 fir	1½	(38)	5½	(140)	10'	(3m)	cut to length and angle
Q	3	deck end framers	2×6 fir	1½	(38)	5½	(140)	20'	(6m)	cut to length and angle

TECH tip

The two-support-post design is simple and attractive, but asks a lot of the posts to carry and support the roof structure. The quality and availability of building materials varies from place to place, as do conditions and building codes. The support posts need to be the right kind for the job, so check with a design professional — architect or engineer — and your local building department to determine the correct material size, grade and depth the posts are to be set into the ground.

1 Planning and layout are important issues. I already had an area dedicated to BBQ-ing, so the question was, what to build? The design I settled on includes a small gable roof on two post supports. I've always liked Japanese gate roofs and used that basic style as my inspiration. I modified the gable top with a secondary upper roof section to vent cooking smoke. Underground wiring provides power for an electrical outlet and overhead lighting. The structure could be entirely freestanding but I chose to surround it with a ground-level deck. The resulting space is great for chef, family and friends alike.

2 The shape and size of my design evolved through careful consideration of the site and the surrounding landscape. When your design is finalized, using stakes and string, set out the shape of the layout. Then mark the layout on the ground with spray paint.

The Modern Propane Barbecue Grill

The barbecue grill has come a long way from the charcoal and lighter fluid days of the past. Although I still like to use charcoal on occasion, the modern propane barbecue grill is usually my weapon of choice. They're available in sizes ranging all the way from small tabletop portables to huge built-in units that rival commercial kitchens. A medium-size, high-end model with a rotisserie and a separate burner plate was ideal for my purposes and good quality was a must. The "Experience" model No. VCS4005 from Vermont Castings' Signature Series definitely fits the bill and is a pleasure to cook on and with. For more information, go to their website, which is listed in the suppliers section in the back of this book.

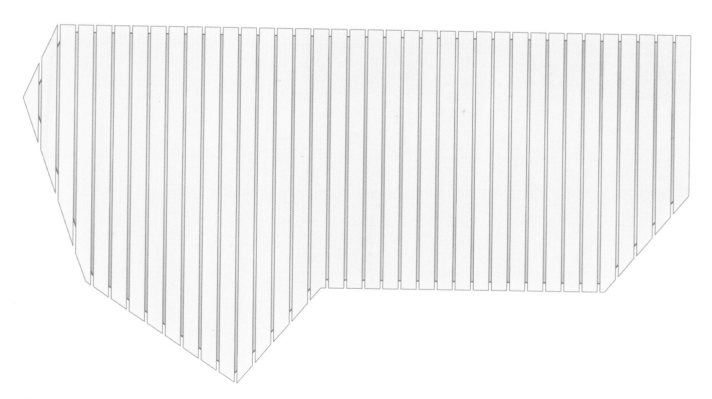

This is how my final deck layout appeared. It offers space for congregating separately from the cooking area.

3 After I had my area layout marked, the first order of business was setting the posts. (See pages 100 and 102 for details on setting posts and using treated lumber.) I used ground-contact treated 6x6 posts set in concrete for the two main supports. Leave them long when you set them and cut them to height when the roof framing is completed. Determine the distance between the posts by what you need to cover. Also, remember to allow ample room for the grill. The materials in this project are combustable.

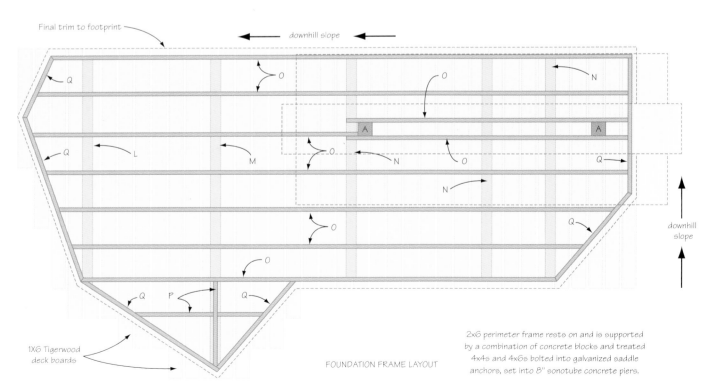

FOUNDATION FRAME LAYOUT

2x6 perimeter frame rests on and is supported
by a combination of concrete blocks and treated
4x4s and 4x6s bolted into galvanized saddle
anchors, set into 8" sonotube concrete piers.

4 The deck framing, for my project, is on the ground at one end. In order to keep the deck level, it gains height above grade toward the other end as the ground slopes away. Use ground-contact treated material for the foundation and the joists.

5 I used a combination of galvanized saddle anchors set in concrete, sonotube piers and concrete blocks to support the deck framing.

6 When all the supports are in place, build the perimeter frame first and then fill in the rest of the joists.

7 With the frame structure complete, put down landscape cloth to keep the weeds and grass out.

8 I used 1×6 tigerwood boards for the decking, spacing them $1/8$" (3mm) apart and fastening them with stainless steel deck screws.

9 I continued laying out the decking boards until the deck was covered.

10 When the decking is in place, snap perimeter chalk lines and cut the finished footprint outline with a circular saw. I suggest using a carbide tipped saw blade for extra blade life.

Which Decking to Use?

Cedar is the traditional choice for decking in my area but it's soft and scars easily. Treated Douglas fir was an option but I wanted something a little dressier. The new synthetic deck materials are increasingly popular but just don't have the look I wanted.

In the end I decided on tigerwood, a tropical hardwood that's tough, has beautiful color and grain and is resistant to rot, water and insect damage. It's available as a certified sustainable forestry product. See the suppliers list for a distributor.

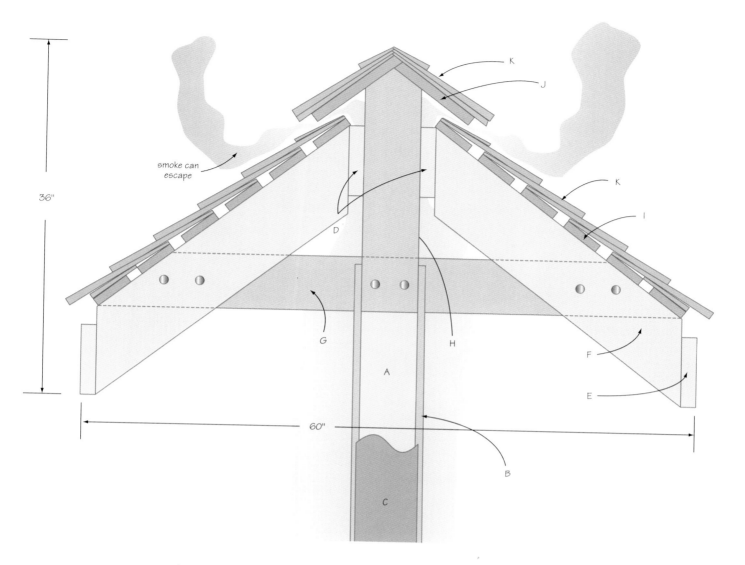

36"

smoke can
escape

K

J

D

H

G

F

E

A

B

C

60"

A standard gable roof has a peak and a ridge cap. I wanted to leave an open gap at the peak to allow cooking smoke to escape but I also wanted to keep the rain out. I accomplished this by building the lower roof section with an open peak and then installing a small secondary-roof-peak structure — essentially a wide, elevated ridge cap — above the opening.

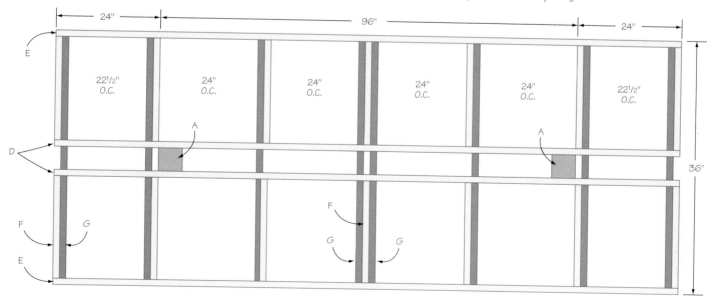

24"

96"

24"

E

22½"
O.C.

24"
O.C.

24"
O.C.

24"
O.C.

24"
O.C.

22½"
O.C.

D

A

A

36"

F

F

G

G

G

F

G

E

LOWER ROOF SECTION RAFTER LAYOUT

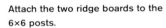

11 Attach the two ridge boards to the 6×6 posts.

12 As an aid for locating the end rafters, attach 2 cross boards to hold the lower roof frame fascia boards temporarily in place.

13 Starting with the end rafters, attach the lower-roof rafters to the ridge boards and attach the facia boards to the ends of the rafters. Then, install the rafter cross ties to the end rafters.

14 Fill in the other rafters and rafter cross ties. Then, starting at each end, install the upper roof supports.

15 Attach the remaining upper roof supports.

16 Install the skip sheathing. Note the extra-length boards clamped to the rafters. Clamp a starter board to these and fit the skip sheathing between it and the upper roof supports.

17 Using the same starter board, layout the first course of shingles. Then install the remaining shingles.

Choice of roofing materials

I chose to use cedar shakes instead of shingles for this project. Going back to my Japanese gate roof concept, I decided that shakes gave a more rustic look to the project. Shakes are more expensive and harder to install, so choose what works best for you. Both cedar shakes or shingles use skip-sheathing underlayment.

Composition shingles are also a good choice for this project. They're less costly and easier to install. Match the proper underlayment (outdoor-rated plywood sheathing) if you choose to use composite shingles.

18 The upper roof supports that project above the lower-roof ridge boards are fitted with 2 upper-roof deck boards. Install these boards.

19 Attach the shakes directly to the upper-roof deck boards.

20 To top it off, install a ridge cap using split shakes laid perpendicular to the roofing shakes.

21 With the roof installation completed, I wrapped the 6×6 posts with rough TK (tight knot) cedar boards. I plan to come back and fill in the open ends of the roof but I want to live with the structure for awhile before I finalize the design. I ran wet-location electrical conduit up from the outlet bo, and installed task lighting under the roof. No more umbrella and headlamp for me!

wooden walkway

6

Most gardens have at least one "transitional" area: a corridor or passageway leading from one part of the garden to another. It's easy to ignore these spaces and their potential is often overlooked and underutilized.

In my garden, a short pathway led between bushes to the worm composting bin and a woodpile beyond. I had always treated it with benign neglect, dismissing it as a necessary means to an end. However, every time it rained the area became a quagmire and I finally realized that something had to change.

This is the space as it looked when I began this project.

I knew that the path was purely functional and wouldn't justify much of an expenditure for landscaping, but I also knew that I didn't want it to be boring and unattractive. I began the search for a design that would be interesting but not flashy, relatively maintenance-free and cost-effective to build. I decided to build a wooden walkway.

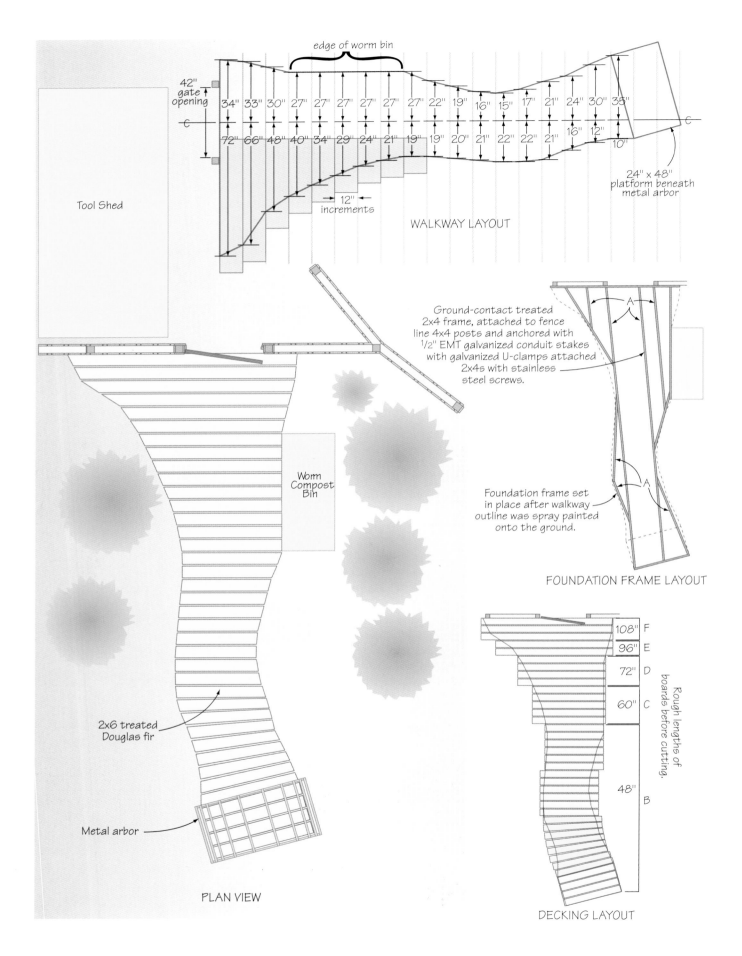

edge of worm bin

42" gate opening

34" 33" 30" 27" 27" 27" 27" 27" 27" 22" 19" 16" 15" 17" 21" 24" 30" 35"

C — — — — — — — — — — — — — — — — — — C

16"

72" 66" 48" 40" 34" 29" 24" 21" 19" 19" 20" 21" 22" 22" 21" 12" 10"

12" increments

WALKWAY LAYOUT

24" x 48" platform beneath metal arbor

Tool Shed

Ground-contact treated 2x4 frame, attached to fence line 4x4 posts and anchored with 1/2" EMT galvanized conduit stakes with galvanized U-clamps attached 2x4s with stainless steel screws.

A

A

Foundation frame set in place after walkway outline was spray painted onto the ground.

FOUNDATION FRAME LAYOUT

Worm Compost Bin

108" F
96" E
72" D
60" C

48" B

Rough lengths of boards before cutting.

2x6 treated Douglas fir

Metal arbor

PLAN VIEW

DECKING LAYOUT

inches (millimeters)

REFERENCE	QUANTITY	PART	STOCK	THICKNESS	(mm)	WIDTH	(mm)	LENGTH (FT)	(m)	COMMENTS
A	*	support frame	treated 2×4	1½	(38)	3½	(89)	*140	(43m)	cut to fit the spray-painted layout
B	24	walkway treads	Douglas fir	1½	(38)	3½	(89)	4	(1.2)	cut to finished length after installation
C	5	walkway treads	Douglas fir	1½	(38)	3½	(89)	5	(1.5)	cut to finished length
D	4	walkway treads	Douglas fir	1½	(38)	3½	(89)	6	(1.8)	cut to finished length
E	2	walkway treads	Douglas fir	1½	(38)	3½	(89)	8	(2.4)	cut to finished length
F	3	walkway treads	Douglas fir	1½	(38)	3½	(89)	9	(2.7)	cut to finished length

1 Before starting the layout, I trenched for the electrical line. The walkway would be used for access to a building that I knew would need electrical power.

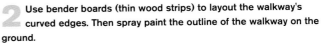

2 Use bender boards (thin wood strips) to layout the walkway's curved edges. Then spray paint the outline of the walkway on the ground.

hardware and supplies

2" (50mm) galvanized nails

½" (13mm) EMT (metal electrical conduit) galvanized stakes

½" (13mm) galvanized conduit clamps

1½" (40mm) stainless steel screws

2" (50mm) deck screws

3 Build, level and anchor the main center section first, then add the smaller outside sections.

4 I anchored the foundation boards with short lengths of $^1/_2$" (13mm) galvanized metal electrical conduit (EMT) driven into the ground and attached to the sides of the boards with galvanized metal conduit clamps and stainless steel screws.

5 Fill in with landscape cloth between the boards. This cloth will prevent the unwanted growing of grass and weeds between the boards.

6 I used above-ground treated Douglas fir 2×6 boards for the walkway treads. My spray-painted edge lines allow me to cut each tread slightly long. Where the walkway curves, the treads need to be tapered. I laid out the curve in place, overlapping the boards to make the curved turn. Then I was able to determine the tapers.

7 I attached a piece of wood to the tread.

8 On the table saw, I cut along the taper line, using the attached strip as a guide against the fence to make the cut.

I love it when a plan comes together!

9 I eased the cut edges with a roundover bit and treated the raw wood with cutoff solution which will prevent moisture from seeping into the wood.

10 Install the treads one at a time using deck screws. Mark with chalk on both ends of each tread where the spray-painted lines show the original layout walkway edges on the soil below.

11 Pressure-treated lumber has an initial high moisture content and it dries over time. When it dries, it shrinks. Install treated deck boards with little or no gap between them. When they dry, a gap will result. Deck boards will also cup as they dry, so install them with the crown of the grain pointed up.

12 Layout the line curves using $1/8" \times 3/4"$ strips of wood and finish nails.

13 Check your layout, fair the curves if necessary and adjust the lines as required. Then mark the line with chalk.

Cut the Curves

The final step in the process was to cut the oversize treads to match my original layout edge lines. The chalk marks I had made on the tread surfaces during installation showed me the edge points of the edge lines, and I used them to mark a cut line along each side of the walkway. Using $1/8" \times 3/4"$ (3mm × 19mm) strips instead of bender board and small finish nails instead of stakes, I laid out the edge lines and curves directly onto the treads and marked them with chalk. I cut along the lines with a jigsaw, using a blade designed to give a smooth finish cut in the 2x material. When all cutting was complete, I eased the edges using a roundover router bit and applied cutoff solution to the raw wood.

14 Cut to the chalk edge lines using a jigsaw. Roundover the cut edges using a router fitted with a roundover bit.

15 Remember to treat the raw ends with cutoff solution. This will help seal the wood against the outdoor elements.

I really enjoyed standing back and appreciating this project when it was completed. A part of my garden that had always existed under the radar had come into its own. My design goals had been met and the result had more than exceeded my expectations. And, best of all, no more muddy feet!

tool shed

7

We've all heard the old saying: "The right tool for the right job." For gardening, I would add: "The right tool for the right job, easy to find, ready to use and stored safely in a well-built tool shed." Tools left out in the weather deteriorate quickly and time spent hunting for tools left scattered throughout the garden is time wasted.

A tool shed doesn't need to be big to provide good storage and the design doesn't have to be complicated. It can be tucked into an out-of-the-way corner of the garden, making good use of underused space. It also can be an architectural feature in its own right.

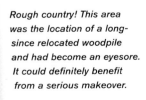

Rough country! This area was the location of a long-since relocated woodpile and had become an eyesore. It could definitely benefit from a serious makeover.

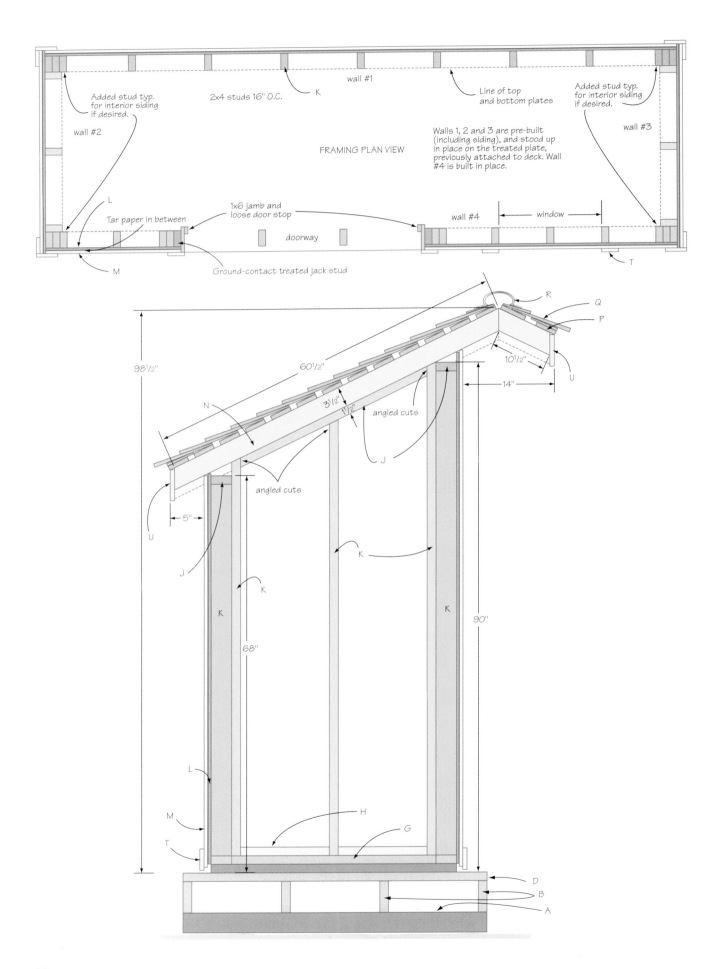

FRAMING PLAN VIEW

wall #1

2x4 studs 16" O.C.

K

Line of top
and bottom plates

Added stud typ.
for interior siding
if desired.

Added stud typ.
for interior siding
if desired.

wall #2

wall #3

Walls 1, 2 and 3 are pre-built
(including siding), and stood up
in place on the treated plate,
previously attached to deck. Wall
#4 is built in place.

L

Tar paper in between

1x6 jamb and
loose door stop

wall #4

window

doorway

M

Ground-contact treated jack stud

T

98 1/2"

60 1/2"

R

Q

P

N

3 1/2"

1 1/2"

angled cuts

10 1/2"

14"

J

U

5"

angled cuts

J

U

K

K

K

K

68"

90"

L

M

T

H

G

D

B

A

inches (millimeters)

REFERENCE	QUANTITY	PART	STOCK	THICKNESS	(mm)	WIDTH	(mm)	LENGTH	(mm)	COMMENTS
4' × 12' DECK										
A	5	support beams	4×4 treated	$3^{1}/_2$	(89)	$3^{1}/_2$	(89)	48	(1219)	
B	4	full-length joists	2×6 treated	$1^{1}/_2$	(38)	$5^{1}/_2$	(140)	141	(3582)	
C	2	end joists	2×6 treated	$1^{1}/_2$	(38)	$5^{1}/_2$	(140)	48	(1219)	
D	27	deck boards	2×6 treated	$1^{1}/_2$	(38)	$5^{1}/_2$	(140)	48	(1219)	
3'8" × 11'2" TOOL SHED										
G	32'	wall baseplates	2×4 treated	$1^{1}/_2$	(38)	$3^{1}/_2$	(89)	*	(*)	*number and lengths as per shed layout
H	32'	wall baseplates	2×4	$1^{1}/_2$	(38)	$3^{1}/_2$	(89)	*	(*)	*number and lengths as per shed layout
J	40'	wall top plates	2×4	$1^{1}/_2$	(38)	$3^{1}/_2$	(89)	*	(*)	*number and lengths as per shed layout
K	35	wall framing studs	2×4	$1^{1}/_2$	(38)	$3^{1}/_2$	(89)	8'	(2.43)	*cut to lengths and angles as required
L	8	wall sheathing	exterior ply	$1/_2$	(13)	4'	(1.22)	8'	(2.43)	8 sheets of plywood, cut to fit as required
M	8	wall siding	cedar ply	$5/_8$	(16)	4'	(1.22)	8'	(2.43)	8 sheets of plywood, cut to fit as required
ROOF										
N	11	rafters	2×4 fir	$1^{1}/_2$	(38)	$3^{1}/_2$	(89)	8'	(2.43)	cut to lengths as required
P	16	skip sheathing	1×3 fir	$3/_4$	(19)	$3^{1}/_2$	(89)	12'	(3.65)	cut to lengths as required
Q	*	roofing	cedar shingles	N/A		N/A		N/A		*verify number of courses per roof layout
R	*	ridge cap	rolled metal	N/A		N/A		N/A		*galvanized rolled metal ridge cap sold in 10' lengths
S	2	ball end cap	galv. metal	N/A		N/A		N/A		for availability, see suppliers list
TRIM										
T	22	trim	1×3 fir	$3/_4$	(19)	$3^{1}/_2$	(89)	8'	(2.43)	cut to lengths as required
U	3	fascia	1×6 fir	$3/_4$	(19)	$5^{1}/_2$	(140)	12'	(3.65)	cut to lengths as required
DOORS										
V	4	stiles	1×4 fir	$3/_4$	(19)	$3^{1}/_2$	(89)	$79^{1}/_2$	(2019)	attached to cedar plywood siding
W	6	rails	1×4 fir	$3/_4$	(19)	$3^{1}/_2$	(89)	$16^{7}/_8$	(429)	attached to cedar plywood siding
X	4	hinge mounts	1×4 fir	$3/_4$	(19)	$3^{1}/_2$	(89)	$3^{1}/_2$	(89)	attached to cedar plywood siding
Y	2	door panels	cedar ply	$5/_8$	(16)	$23^{7}/_8$	(606))	$79^{1}/_2$	(2019)	

hardware and supplies

6 strap hinges for doors, your choice of style

1 door latch

2" (50mm) deck screws

3" (75mm) deck screws

coated framing nails

Planning and Layout

For my tool shed, I chose a simple design with a shed roof. The site I wanted to use was sloped, so I built a platform large enough for the shed and a deck in front of the shed. Then I built the shed directly on top of this platform. This gave me additional useful space around the shed and did not involve a great deal more work than building directly on the ground. (Local building codes and requirements will determine where your shed may be located and what type of foundation should be used. Always check with your building department before starting construction!) I brought in underground power for lighting and an outdoor electrical outlet and included a window in the design just because I liked the way it looked.

1 At one end of the deck framing I hung the joists on a ledger I installed on an adjacent outbuilding.

2 At the other end I attached a rim joist to a line of 4×4 fence posts set in concrete.

3 I attached the two side rim joists and installed two 4×4 intermediate supports beneath them.

Note to readers:

The materials list for this project includes only enough stock to build a deck large enough to accommodate the tool shed. I built a larger deck to create extra space around my shed. This project is intended to give you some ideas about how you could possibly use the available space around your shed.

4 I put down landscape cloth, filling in between the intermediate joists. I built the main rectangular section of the footprint first and framed the small triangular corner. I also fitted a 4×4 post for a future railing.

5 I used above-ground treated Douglas fir 2×6 boards for the decking. After checking the layout math to determine the width of the final decking board, I cut the boards slightly long and set them loosely in place. Then I marked and drilled a hole for the electrical wire. Next I snapped chalk lines across the boards to indicate the joists below and attached the decking with deck screws. Finally, I snapped the perimeter edge lines and cut the boards to finished lengths using a circular saw.

6 With the deck in place, I was ready to build the shed. The decking served as the shed floor, so the walls could be attached directly to the surface. I installed a base plate of treated lumber to keep the untreated wall framing up off the deck and to serve as a location guide during installation.

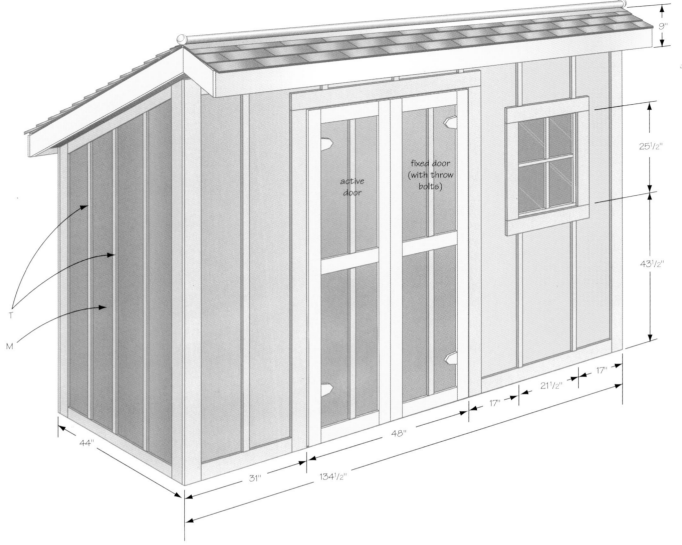

9"

25½"

43½"

active door

fixed door (with throw bolts)

T

M

44"

31"

134½"

48"

17"

21½"

17"

7 I built the back and side walls as complete sections, using the deck as my worksurface.

8 The siding layers can now be installed.

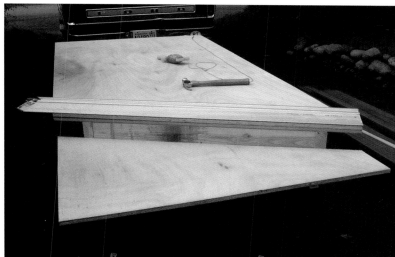

10 Build the side walls, cut the siding to fit and install it.

9 With the siding attached, raise the back wall into place and nail it to the base plate.

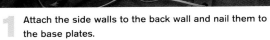

12 With the back and side walls in place, frame the front wall and install the siding.

11 Attach the side walls to the back wall and nail them to the base plates.

13 Apply an outdoor preservative stain to the outer siding.

14 Install the rafters.

15 Attach the fascia boards.

16 I installed the side fiscia boards a little long and cut them to fit.

17 To give the roof some breathability, install skip sheathing. Then attach the cedar shingles using a 5" reveal.

18 Finish off the roof with a rolled galvanized roof cap with ball ends. This adds a nice old-fashioned touch to the shed.

19 With the roof attached, it's time to install the trim. I started with the outside corners and moved to the window and doors. Wrap some roofing felt around the corners to seal the siding joints against the weather.

20 Make the four outside corner trim caps. Using galvanized nails or stainless-steel staples, install the caps over the felt-paper seals.

21 Remember to keep the bottoms of the trim caps $1/2$" (13mm) above the deck's surface. This will keep moisture from soaking up into the trim and rotting it.

22 The door casing is installed just like a traditional door. Remember to use cedar shims since it's outdoors.

Save a window?

I wanted a small window in the shed but I didn't need a fancy new one. A used window — from a remodel or builder's salvage yard — can be repaired and reused. In this case it was the perfect choice.

I needed to replace the top and bottom rails. Use waterproof glue to attach the new pieces.

Remove the excess dried glue, prime, paint and you're ready to install.

You'd never guess this was a used window. It was a great choice.

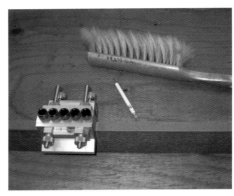

23 The doors are made in two parts. A face-frame assemby and a plywood siding backer. Make the face frames using dowels and waterproof glue.

24 Assemble the frames and pre-paint them. Then, using panel adhesive and stainless-steel screws, attach the face frames to the plywood siding.

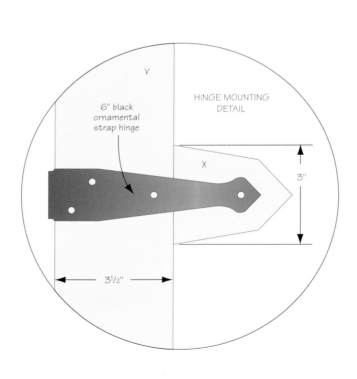

6" black ornamental strap hinge

HINGE MOUNTING DETAIL

X

3"

3½"

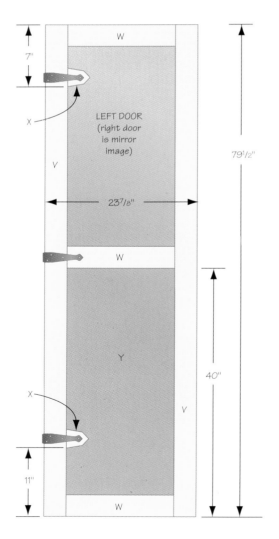

W

7"

X

LEFT DOOR (right door is mirror image)

V

23⅞"

W

79½"

W

Y

40"

X

V

11"

W

25 The hinges and latches are barn-door hardware. The hinges are mounted on decorative backer pieces where they extend past the face frame. Be sure to fit the doors before installing the hinges. If you attach the hinges first, you may need to remove the doors a time or two to fit them.

26 I installed some battens on each door that match the battens on the rest of the tool shed.

The final result is great – a place for everything. I added couple of wide steps, two short railing sections at the edge of the deck to improve access, safety and a couple of chairs in case a short break is required now and then. Now if I can just work on the self-discipline to put everything in its place...

trellis with paving stones

8

A garden is a wonderful place for relaxation, contemplation and the appreciation of nature. Personally, I tend to do these things best while sitting down and traditional landscape architecture proves that I am not alone. The Romans favored cool marble grottos, Europeans built elaborate structures of wood and metal, oriental gardens feature beautifully integrated seating made of wood and stone,and Americans have experimented with any and everything, including willow branches, plastic, wood, canvas and concrete. No matter what the culture, garden design has always provided a good place to sit.

Garden seating, however, should be more than just utilitarian. Whether simple or elaborate, it should harmonize with its surroundings, integrated into both the landscaping and nearby structures. It should be solid and well built, but not overbuilt. It should fit the site and reflect the sensibilities of the designer and builder.

A trellis over a bench or loveseat can meet all these criteria. It is satisfying both to build and to use and is a perfect project for amateur and professional woodworkers alike. Starting with a simple, basic framework, I'll show you a straightforward, step-by-step construction plan. Along the way, I'll suggest how you can personalize the design to meet your individual needs and requirements. By mixing and matching materials, top details and side panel construction, you can create a unique structure that will be the focal point of your garden.

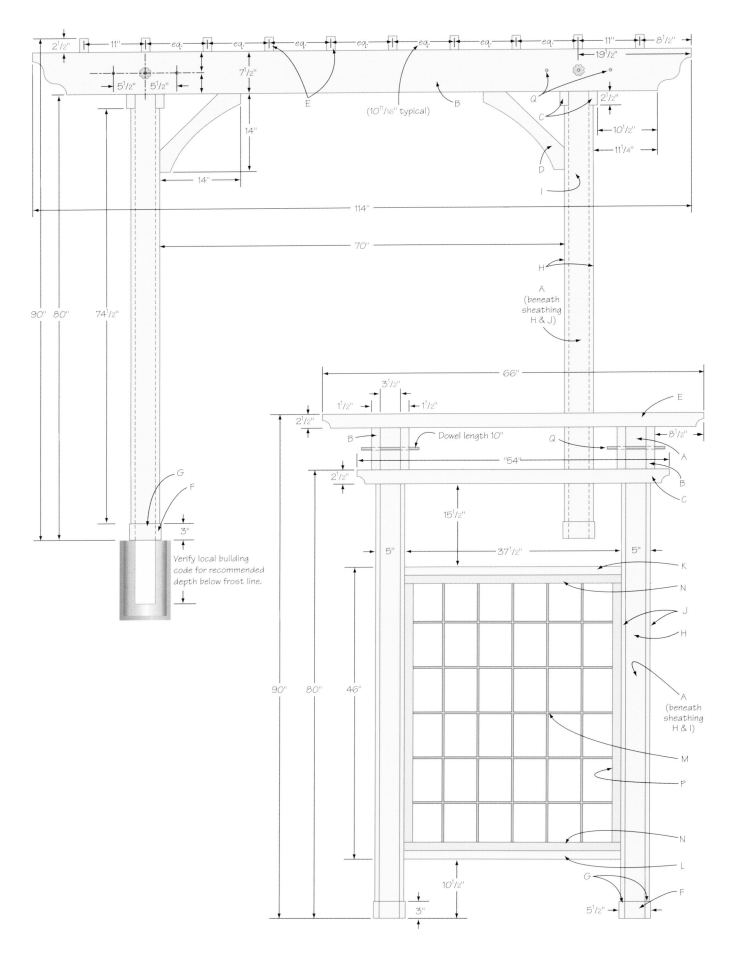

2 1/2" 11" eq. eq. eq. eq. eq. eq. eq. eq. 11" 8 1/2"

19 1/2"

7 1/2"

5 1/2" 5 1/2"

14"

E

(10 11/16" typical) B

Q

C

2 1/2"

10 1/2"

11 1/4"

D

I

14"

114"

70"

H

A
(beneath
sheathing
H & J)

90" 80" 74 1/2"

G

F

3"

Verify local building
code for recommended
depth below frost line.

66"

3 1/2"

1 1/2" 1 1/2"

2 1/2"

E

B Dowel length 10" Q

8 1/2"

"54"

A

B

C

2 1/2"

15 1/2"

5" 37 1/2" 5"

K

N

J

H

90" 80" 46"

A
(beneath
sheathing
H & I)

M

P

N

L

G

F

10 1/2"

3"

5 1/2"

inches (millimeters)

REFERENCE	QUANTITY	PART	STOCK	THICKNESS	(mm)	WIDTH	(mm)	LENGTH	(mm)	COMMENTS
A	4	posts/uprights	treated lumber	3^1/$_2$	(89)	3^1/$_2$	(89)	10'	(3m)	set in concrete, cut to length
B	4	main beams	red cedar	1^1/$_2$	(38)	7^1/$_2$	(191)	114	(2.9m)	install rough side to the front or outside
C	4	cross beams	red cedar	1^1/$_2$	(38)	2^1/$_2$	(64)	54	(1372)	
D	4	knee braces	red cedar	1^1/$_2$	(38)	5^1/$_2$	(140)	24	(610)	
E	10	roof crosspieces	red cedar	1^1/$_2$	(38)	2^1/$_2$	(64)	66	(1676)	
F	8	narrow plinth block bases	red cedar	1	(25)	3^1/$_2$	(89)	3	(76)	install rough side out
G	8	wide plinth block bases	red cedar	1	(25)	5	(127)	3	(76)	install rough side out
H	8	narrow post sheath boards	red cedar	^{3}/$_4$	(19)	3^1/$_2$	(89)	74^1/$_2$	(1893)	install rough side out
J	8	wide post sheath boards	red cedar	^{3}/$_4$	(19)	4^1/$_2$	(115)	77	(1956)	install rough side out, notch both sides of the top
K	2	side panel top rails	red cedar	1^1/$_2$	(38)	3^1/$_2$	(89)	37^1/$_2$	(953)	
L	2	side panel bottom rails	red cedar	1^1/$_2$	(38)	3^1/$_2$	(89)	37^1/$_2$	(953)	groove along the center of the top ^{1}/$_4$"-deep by ^{1}/$_2$"-wide, drill weep holes in the bottom
M	2	side panels	galvanized "pig wire" fence panels			36	(914)	48	(1219)	should have 6" × 8" wire o.c. openings
N	8	panel horizontal stops	red cedar	1	(25)	1^1/$_2$	(38)	37^1/$_2$	(953)	
P	8	panel vertical stops	red cedar	1	(25)	1^1/$_2$	(38)	46	(1168)	
Q	8	dowel rods	teak	^{1}/$_2$	(38)			10	(254)	chamfer both ends slightly
R	8	brace spacer	copper plumbing tube	^{3}/$_4$	(19)			1	(25)	

hardware and supplies

^{5}/$_8$" × 8" (16mm × 200mm) galvanized bolts with galvanized maleable washers and galvanized split washers and nuts

^{3}/$_8$" × 3" (10mm × 75mm) galvanized lag screws

^{1}/$_2$" × 6" (13mm × 150mm) galvanized lag screws with galvanized maleable washers

^{5}/$_{16}$" × 4" (8mm × 100mm) galvanized lag screws

4" (100mm) galvanized spikes

2" (50mm) galvanized box nails

1^1/$_2$" (40mm) galvanized box nails

3" (75mm) galvanized finish nails

2^1/$_2$" (65mm) galvanized box nails

Galvanized indicates "hot-dipped galvanized." Stainless could be substituted.

Before Construction

My backyard slopes gradually and the top end is a logical place to have seating that overlooks the garden. A couple of chairs and a loveseat have served over the years but were not very exciting. The area was obviously underutilized and I always knew that a small trellis over a bench or loveseat would be a great addition.

It's important to consider the site carefully when developing your design. In my case, I needed to be sure that the structure wouldn't block too much sunlight from the surrounding plants. I also wanted the design to be open enough to allow views of trees, shrubs and flowers through the structure, but still to be friendly to climbing vines and other plants. Finally, I wanted the general design and materials to complement the design of the house and other garden structures and features.

Designing the Structure

Settling on a final design that feels and looks right can be more than a little intimidating with so many details and options to consider. I tend to be a visual person and have found that photographs and drawings can be an invaluable resource. A few evenings of quality time spent looking through books and magazine back issues at the public library can greatly expand your design horizons and help you identify design elements that work for you.

Following the "simple is better" theory, I chose to use pressure-treated 4×4s set in concrete for the four corner support posts. I like the look of rough western red cedar (and had already used it for fence boards in the garden), so I used it to wrap the pressure-treated posts. I also used rough-one-side, tight-knot western red

cedar for the 2×8 top beams (both for the look and for the significant cost savings compared to clear grade). For the rest of the structural pieces I used clear, surfaced-four-sides western red cedar, which I hand-selected for color and grain. The design of the various beam, support and trellis board ends and spacing was purely my individual

choice, the result of trial-and-error design and layout. The design of the side panels took into account my requirements for light, views and providing open structure for climbing plants.

Building the Structure
Mark the Location of the Four Support Posts

Twenty years' experience as a carpenter and cabinetmaker has taught me the importance of good planning and accurate layout. A little time spent wrestling with the details at the beginning of a project will yield fewer design errors and greatly increase construction efficiency. The first step in this project is to set the footprint for the structure and make sure that the corners are square.

The traditional method for laying out a square or rectangular footprint with 90° corners involves batter boards, string lines, a plumb bob, a measuring tape and it usually requires two people. This works well, but is a bit excessive for this project. I use a different method for smaller projects that is simple, fast, very accurate and can be done by one person working alone.

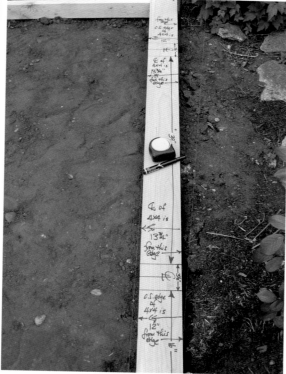

2 Measure and mark the 4x4 post locations and centerline on the frame sides.

1 Here's where careful layout comes into play. Using the footprint like a piece of graph paper, measure both ways from each corner and mark the exact locations and center lines of the four 4×4 posts on all four sides of the frame. Precision layout of the post locations ensures that the distances between them are accurate and to plan. This will make cutting and installing the other parts fast and efficient. Using 2×4s and duplex nails, build a frame that's a bit larger than the footprint of the structure. Position the front corners first and set them in place with stakes. Then, measuring from corner to opposing corner, adjust the back edge back and forth until the two measurements are equal. This shows that the four corners are square and the frame is a true rectangle. After staking the back corners in place, you're ready to begin the layout for setting the posts.

3 Set duplex nails at the center line markings on all four frame sides. Stringing lines from nail to nail, make a grid cross-pattern that exactly locates the centers of the four posts.

4 Using the crossed lines as a guide, spray-paint the center locations of the posts on the dirt below. When the lines are removed, the marks show exactly where to dig the postholes.

Dig the Holes and Set the Posts in Concrete

Methods of Setting Posts

The four corner posts are the basis for the entire structure. Properly installed, they not only support the rest of the structure but prevent the settling, shifting and buckling that can result from seasonal temperature changes, wind and weather. It's important to set them correctly, in holes of the proper depth.

The depth of the hole depends on your location's frost line – the depth below ground level to which the soil will freeze in cold weather. (Your local building department should be able to give you this information.) If the bottom of the hole does not extend below this depth, ice can form under the bottom of the post and footing, pushing it upward and weakening and distorting the structure, a process called frost heave.

Once the hole is dug, the pressure-treated post is set plumb in the center of the hole. It can be held firmly in place using one of the following methods:

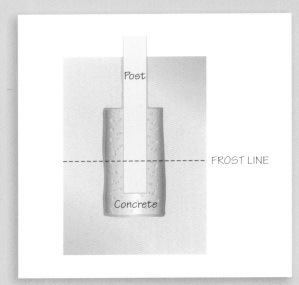

METHOD ONE
CONCRETE IN HOLE

Dig a hole to the proper depth with a post hole digger. Make the bottom of the hole a bit wider than the shaft to provide an additional anchor and to discourage uplift. Throw a few small rocks in the bottom of the hole and tamp down firmly. Set the post plumb in the center of the hole with temporary braces and fill the hole with concrete to about 4" (100mm) to 6" (150mm) below the grade of the bottom of the future surface.

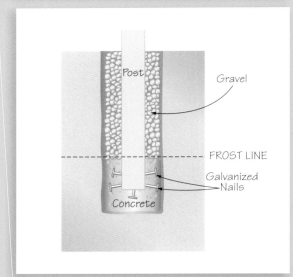

METHOD TWO
CONCRETE & GRAVEL IN HOLE

Dig a hole to the proper depth with a post hole digger. Make the bottom of the hole slightly wider than the shaft to provide an additional anchor and discourage uplift. Tamp down the bottom of the hole firmly. Drive a few galvanized nails partially into the bottom of the post. Put some concrete into the bottom of the hole — enough to cover the nails when the post is set in place. Set the post in the center of the hole with the nails embedded in the concrete and brace to plumb. Fill the hole with gravel and tamp in place.

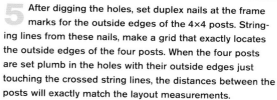

5 After digging the holes, set duplex nails at the frame marks for the outside edges of the 4×4 posts. Stringing lines from these nails, make a grid that exactly locates the outside edges of the four posts. When the four posts are set plumb in the holes with their outside edges just touching the crossed string lines, the distances between the posts will exactly match the layout measurements.

6 The four corner posts are AP treated 4×4×10s. Leave them long when setting and cut the tops off to length before attaching the beams. Set one post first and use it as a reference for setting the other three. Use a post level to plumb the post. When both bubbles read true with the outside edges of the post just touching the crossed string lines, set two angled 2×2 braces to hold it in place and pour premixed concrete into the hole. Let the concrete cure overnight. Then, move on to the other three posts.

Not All Treated Lumber is Created Equal

Using treated wood for the posts is an obvious choice, since they will be set in holes below grade, in contact with soil and concrete. However, it's important to use lumber that has received the proper level of treatment.

Wood that will be used outdoors is routinely treated with a chemical preservative that is forced deep into the wood fibers in a high-pressure tank. Different levels of treatment (standards set by the American Wood Preservers Association) are measured according to the retention level of the preservative in the finished product. The retention level is defined as pounds of preservative per cubic foot (pcf) of wood product.

All pressure-treated lumber will have a tag stapled to one end that shows a wealth of information: the brand name, name of the wood treatment facility, AWPA standards, type of preservative used, retention level, third-party inspector and end-use application.

The important information for most of us is the retention level and the corresponding end-use designation:

0.10 pcf	Decking
0.25 pcf	Above Ground
0.40 pcf	Ground Contact
0.60 pcf	Permanent Wood Foundation (PWF)
2.50 pcf	Salt Water

Pressure-treated wood is significantly more corrosive to metal fasteners than untreated (five times more corrosive to common steel according to AWPA testing), so choose fasteners accordingly. For this project, hot-dipped galvanized or stainless steel will suffice.

If the chemical soup used to treat lumber can dissolve steel, think what it might do to you! Use common safety sense when working with this material.

- Use a dust mask and eye protection. Avoid skin contact whenever possible.
- Collect sawdust and dispose of sawdust and offcuts properly. Use a tarp under the work area to make cleanup easier and to limit the migration of sawdust onto lawns and flower beds.
- Never burn pressure-treated wood. In addition to the possibility of toxic smoke, the ash created may also contain toxic chemical residue.

7 Set the other three posts in their holes just like the first, with outside edges just touching the crossed string lines. Also make some simple spacers (sized to match the layout measurements between the posts) that you can clamp to the posts at eye level or a bit higher. After checking for plumb with the post level and setting angled braces, pour the concrete into the holes and let it cure at least overnight before proceeding.

8 With the grunt work completed, the fun can begin. The main components of the upper structure are four 2×8 beams that connect the 4×4 posts: two across the back and two across the front. The beams and the beam-ends are like a blank slate — here's where you can start to make the design your own. Whether you prefer simple Zen-inspired angled cuts or lean more toward rococo swirls, artistic license is the name of the game. The first step is to temporarily set the front beam in place. Clamp a 2×2 from front to back across the two posts at each end of the structure, set and leveled so that the top of each 2×2 is at the proposed height of the bottom of the beam. Then set the beam in place and clamp each end to its post. With the beam held safely in place, you're free to experiment with design ideas.

Examples of Beam End Designs

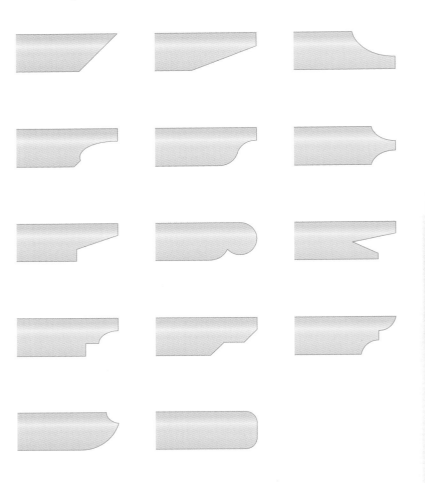

TECH tip

Sometimes it's hard to tell from a drawing just how a design will look in real life. When I've whittled down my choices to a final few, I make full-scale patterns out of 1/2" (13mm)-thick plywood that I can clamp to the beam and actually see in place. This helps me make my final decision.

Making a Pattern

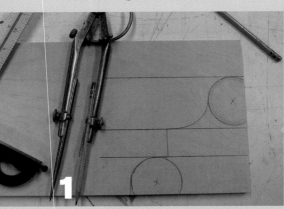

1

Get it right. Accurate pattern layout is important.

2

Let the tools do the work. A drill press and a hole saw do a much better job than cutting freehand with a jigsaw. Neatness counts.

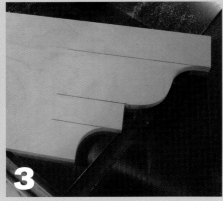

3

A pattern to be proud of. Now you can see the real thing.

9 Once you've decided on a beam-end, it's time to start woodworking. Transferring the pattern design accurately to the actual beams is easy if you use a few simple tricks. Start by laying the pattern on another 1/2" (13mm)-thick plywood pattern blank, making sure that the edges representing the beam end are flush. Remove the hole saw from the drill press and loosen the pilot bit fixing screw, then carefully set the hole saw in place where it originally cut one of the pattern holes. Give the pilot bit a tap with a hammer. This acts like a center punch, transferring the starter hole location accurately to the blank. Repeat the procedure to mark the second starter hole. After resetting the pilot bit in the hole saw with the fixing screw and chucking the hole saw back in the drill press, drill starter holes just through the two marked locations on the blank pattern, making sure that the hole saw does not cut through the plywood. Then clamp the new starter hole pattern to one end of the actual beam and, using a drill bit the same size as the hole saw starter bit, drill two starter holes all the way through the beam. Repeat the procedure at the opposite end and the beam is ready to have the pattern holes cut.

10 Although it's possible to cut saw holes using a hand-held drill motor, I prefer to use the drill press, for two reasons. First, it's safer: hole saws are pretty aggressive tools and catching an edge can result in a rude awakening at best or even a broken wrist. Second, it results in a cleaner hole. Run the hole about two-thirds of the way through the board from one side and turn the board over to finish the cut. This prevents tear-out that can occur when the hole saw is run all the way through the board and also makes it easier to remove the plug from the saw. (Some hole saws have a limited depth capacity, so you'll need to do this anyway to cut through 2x stock.) Horsing a long beam around on the drill press can be awkward, so always support the loose end and clamp the working end securely to the table.

11 Start the hole on one side, then turn the board over to finish. The two accurate holes make cutting the rest of the pattern a snap. Two small cuts with a jigsaw, some cleanup with a sander and the job is done. I chose to run a small cove detail using a $\frac{3}{8}$" (10mm) radius bit to dress up the edges. The result: four identical finished beams, ready for installation.

12 Finish the pattern with a jigsaw and clean up the cuts with a sander.

13 Rout a decorative edge detail.

14 Here are the completed beam ends.

Cut the Post Tops to Length

Since the posts were left long when they were set in the holes, they'll need to be cut to finished length before the beams are attached. I cut a pointed-top "gable" profile using a circular saw set for an angled cut and treated the raw wood with an offcut solution to provide weather protection. I made the cuts using blocks clamped to the posts to support and guide the saw base and to allow accurate measurement. I planned the post top to sit slightly below the top of the beams (purely a personal design decision) and sloped the cuts so that water will drain out the open sides and not collect against the beams.

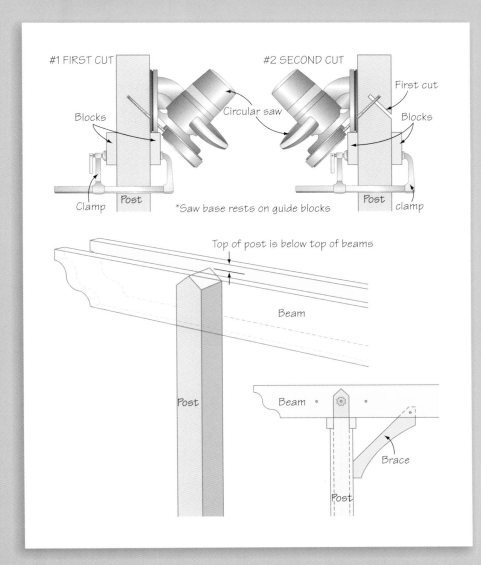

After careful measurements and layout, position and clamp blocks to opposite sides of the post to guide the cuts. Leave the blocks long on both ends to provide good support for the saw base at the start and the end of each cut. Cut one side. Then cut the opposite side. The two cuts should intersect, leaving a nicely pointed top.

The post top sits slightly below the top of the beams, with the angled cuts sloping away from the sides of the beams.

(safety tip)

If you're not careful, the waste piece above the top will "jump" as the saw finishes the second cut and the scrap — now unconnected and unsupported — suddenly comes in contact with the spinning blade. It's much safer to stop the second cut short and finish the last bit with a hand saw.

15 Before installing the beams, cut off the posts so the tops won't show above the upper edges. With the beams clamped in place front and back on the posts, drill a $^9/_{16}$" (14mm) hole all the way through each corner's pair of beams and the post between them. Bolt each corner assembly together using a $^1/_2$" (13mm) galvanized bolt, washers, lock washer and nut. You can also use galvanized malleable washers for a design accent. With the beams bolted in place, the 2×2s can be removed. To tie the front and back posts together, use 2×3 clear cedar braces. Here's another place where some detail can really dress up the design. Use the same hole saw you used for the beam pattern to make a cove detail at the ends and the same router cove detail around all edges. Bolt the completed 2×3s directly to the 4×4 posts below the beams using galvanized $^5/_{16}$" (8mm) lag screws and washers.

Through-Section Showing Post and Sheathing

Once the front and back 2×3 braces were attached, I sheathed the exposed APT posts with rough 1x cedar. I used 1×4 boards for the sides and ripped 1×5 boards to 4$^1/_2$" (114mm)-wide for the fronts and backs. This covers the seam where post and 1x3 meet and leaves a stepped $^1/_4$" (6mm) reveal on each side. I notched the upper corners so the top will fit between the 2×3s and meet the bottom of the beam above and ran a small router cove detail along the edges. I left the sheathing well above grade to prevent ground contact and possible rot. I'll install a rough cedar plinth base around each post after the paving stones are installed beneath the structure.

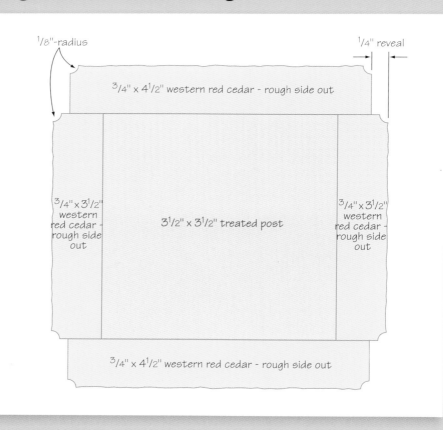

$^1/_8$"-radius

$^1/_4$" reveal

$^3/_4$" x 4$^1/_2$" western red cedar - rough side out

$^3/_4$" x 3$^1/_2$" western red cedar - rough side out

3$^1/_2$" x 3$^1/_2$" treated post

$^3/_4$" x 3$^1/_2$" western red cedar - rough side out

$^3/_4$" x 4$^1/_2$" western red cedar - rough side out

Examples of Diagonal Brace Designs

Corner braces aren't required for a structure of this small size, but they can add another level of architectural detail to the project. I chose to make a fairly simple angled brace, slightly curved along the bottom edge, from 2×6 clear cedar. Attached at the bottom to the post by a countersunk galvanized lag screw, each brace extends up between the beams and is attached from behind the back beam with a long galvanized lag screw.

Constructing Bracing

I chose this brace design for three reasons: (1) it is an interesting design without being too gaudy; (2) it's pretty straightforward to construct and install and (3) the top attachment detail between the main beams provides flowers and vines a good place to climb.

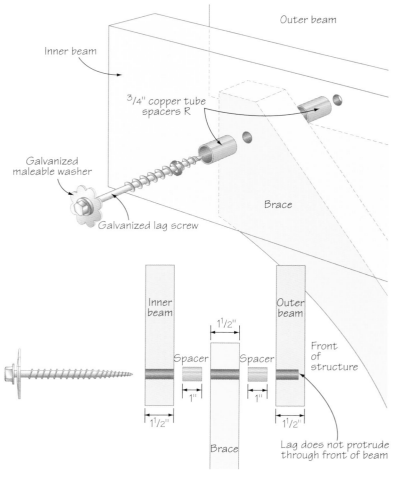

Outer beam

Inner beam

3/4" copper tube spacers R

Galvanized maleable washer

Galvanized lag screw

Brace

Inner beam

Outer beam

1 1/2"

Spacer

Spacer

Front of structure

1"

1"

1 1/2"

1 1/2"

Brace

Lag does not protrude through front of beam

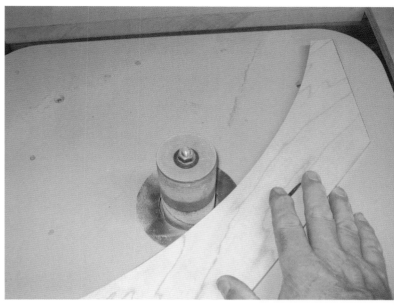

16 First, make a pattern template out of scrap ½" (13mm)-thick plywood. After ripping it to width and cutting the end angles, set the curve by bowing a thin strip of clear wood and marking the resulting line with a marker.

17 Cut away the waste and fair the curve using a belt or drum sander.

18 Using the pattern, mark the curve onto the cedar stock and cut away the waste to within ⅛" (3mm) of the line. Fairing the curve on thick stock by sanding is difficult — not to mention inaccurate. A more reliable way is to trim the last ⅛" (3mm) using a router and a pattern-cutting top-bearing bit, using the plywood pattern as a template guide.

19 Temporarily attach the template to the stock using small, removable brads or double-sided tape.

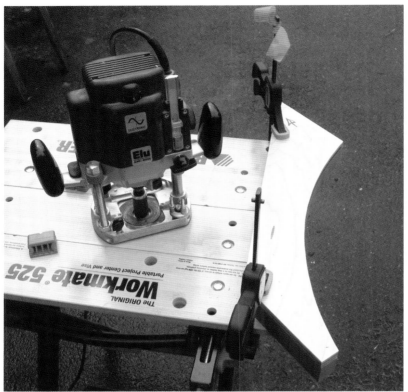

20 Clamp the work piece securely to a stable work surface.

21 The router bit bearing can guide the cutter exactly along the pattern curve. This makes it easy to cut all four braces exactly the same.

22 A trimmer or small router with a bottom-bearing guide cuts a decorative cove detail along the edges.

23 Predrill and countersink the bottom of the brace.

24 Attach the brace to the center of the post with a galvanized lag screw.

25 The top of the brace is attached from behind the back of the rear main beam with a long galvanized lag screw into the back of the front main beam. The galvanized malleable washer is only for decoration.

26 The brace is centered between the pair of main beams using two short, equal lengths of $3/4''$ (19mm) copper plumbing tubing that house the lag screw and act as rigid spacers.

Build and Install the Side Panels

Examples of Side Panel Designs

Next to the beams, the side panels are the most important design element of the structure. Here again, careful planning at the start of the project will pay off. Whether you choose to use traditional lattice or decide to go free form with modern materials, the procedure for installing the panels is the same.

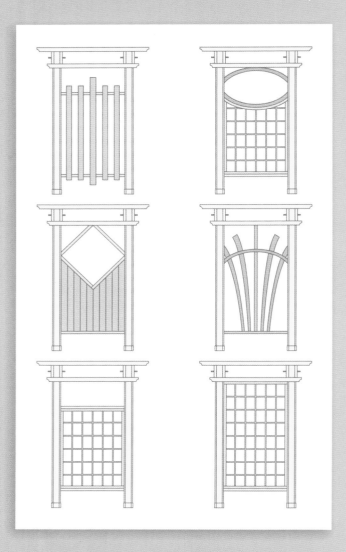

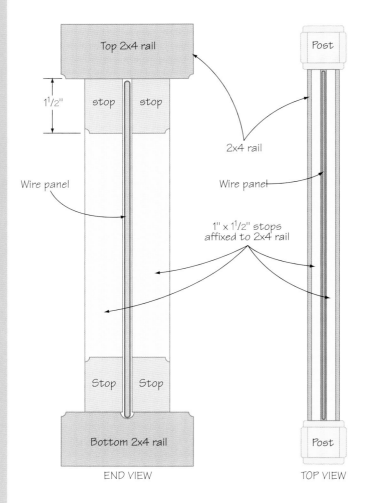

END VIEW

TOP VIEW

For my side panels, I chose a heavy-gauge galvanized wire mesh with 6" × 8" (150mm × 200mm) openings. (This is used for farm and barnyard fencing and is available through farm supply dealers and co-ops.) This gives me the open feeling I require for the location, lets the sunlight through to the plants beyond and provides a great trellis for climbing plants. I left a good-size opening above the panel for the same reasons. I used cedar 2×4s as the top and bottom structural pieces to house the panels and stopped the panels in on all four sides with 5/4×2 cedar strips and galvanized nails. I again routed a small cove detail along the edges. Careful layout at the beginning of the project ensures that the panel and opening dimensions are the same and the stops are easy to cut and install.

Let it Drain

The stops along the bottom rail hold the wire panel in place, but they can also capture and hold rain and moisture, leading eventually to rot. There's an easy fix for this potential problem.

When installed, the wire panel is centered in the groove above the weep holes, which allows rain and moisture to drain.

Before installing the bottom rail, rout a groove approximately $1/2$" (13mm) wide by $1/4$" (6mm) deep along the top of the 2×4. Drill "weep holes" through the board every 4" (100mm) on center in the groove.

Examples of Top Trellis Designs

The final step is to design and install the top trellis pieces. I went with my basic design theme and used 2×3 clear cedar with the same details as the 2×3 braces below the beams. The layout was purely arbitrary; I simply experimented until it felt right. I made plywood layout templates that I clamped to the outside of the front and rear beams to make the installation accurate and attached the pieces to the tops of the beams with galvanized nails.

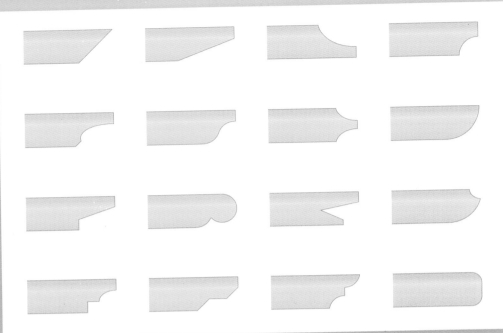

27 Use a layout template to accurately position the pieces on the beams.

28 Attach the trellis pieces using galvanized nails.

Paving Stone Surface

With the trellis completed, the next step is to provide a good, durable surface for a bench or loveseat. I looked for low-maintenance, weatherproof materials that would complement and enhance the overall design of the project. I also wanted a product that wouldn't require too much cutting or modification to fit into the available space and footprint.

hardware and supplies

5" × 5¾" (125mm × 145mm) Paleo Pavers mixed precast concrete (random pattern)

5¾" × 5¾" (145mm × 145mm) Paleo Pavers mixed precast concrete (random pattern)

7¼" × 5¾" (185mm × 145mm) Paleo Pavers mixed precast concrete (random pattern)

I used 165 stones.

6" (150mm) exposed aggregate concrete curb

builder's sand

base gravel

landscape fabric

6 pc.   7' (215cm) lengths plastic paver edging, cut to fit

12" (305mm) galvanized spikes

Examples of Pavers and Patterns

After considering options as varied as exposed aggregate concrete, wood decking, gauged slate tiles and brick, I decided to use precast concrete paving blocks. I chose a style that features three different sizes: all are the same thickness and length but have different widths. This allowed me to mix and match the blocks to form a random side-to-side pattern, while keeping the front-to-back courses equal and easier to lay out. It also gave me three sizes to choose from when a curved edge required cutting the block to fit. The edges and corners of the blocks are slightly rough and rounded, giving a rustic look that fits the overall design.

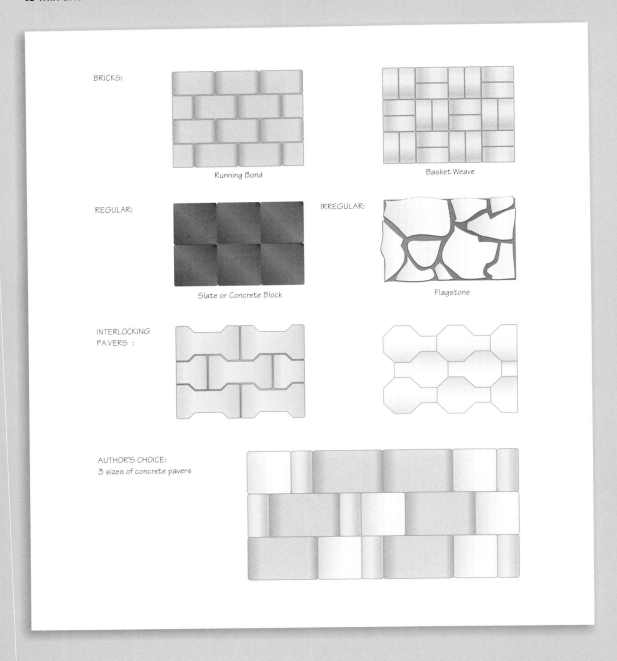

BRICKS:

Running Bond

Basket Weave

REGULAR:

Slate or Concrete Block

IRREGULAR:

Flagstone

INTERLOCKING PAVERS :

AUTHOR'S CHOICE:
3 sizes of concrete pavers

Build It to Last

A base built from paving blocks — even without mortared joints — can be almost as strong as a solid surface. Starting from the ground up, the key elements for sound construction are: a good base, a tight fit and proper installation. The tried-and-true method takes a multilayered approach: paver blocks are set into a layer of sand over a layer of gravel over landscape cloth over compacted earth. The pavers are initially set slightly higher (approximately 1" [25mm]) than the finish level and then tamped — either by hand with a block and mallet or using a mechanical compactor — down into the sand layer to finish grade. During the tamping process, sand is broomed into the joints to further set the pavers solidly in place.

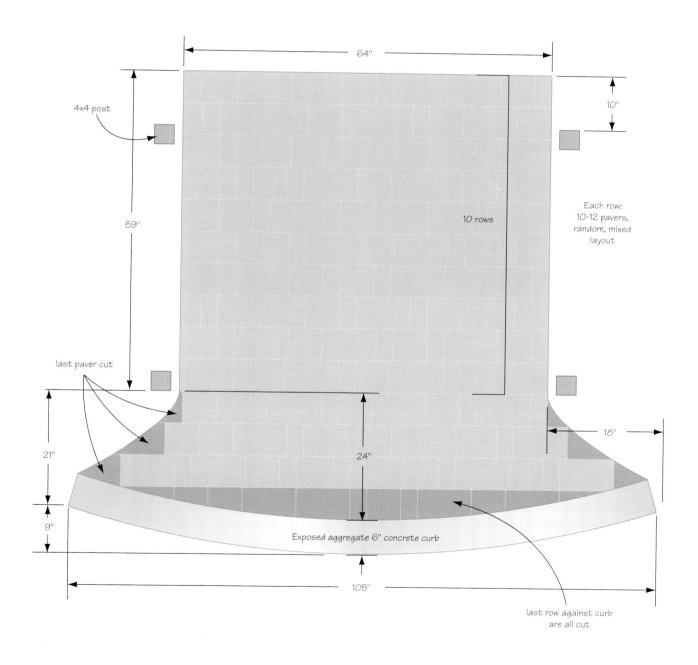

4x4 post

64"

10"

59"

10 rows

Each row:
10-12 pavers,
random, mixed
layout

last paver cut

21"

24"

18"

9"

Exposed aggregate 6" concrete curb

105"

last row against curb
are all cut

29 To determine how far down to dig (the excavation grade level), it's necessary to first determine where the top surface of the pavers (the finish surface grade level) will be. Using one side of my front curb as a starting point, I clamped and tacked level temporary perimeter boards to the outside of the structure posts. The bottoms of these boards are at the finish surface grade level: the exact level of the paving block surface.

30 The next step is to dig out below the finish grade level down to the excavation grade level. A depth gauge made from wood and plywood makes accurately establishing the excavation grade level a snap. The gauge's top board rests on top of the perimeter boards and the narrower plywood center section below shows the excavation grade level (the height of the perimeter board plus the excavation depth required below the finish grade level). As you dig, move the depth gauge along the side perimeter boards to determine when you reach the excavation grade level.

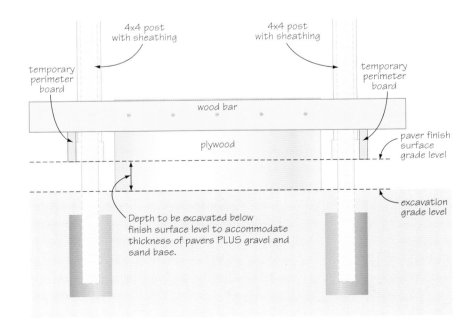

31 A flat-ended spade works well for leveling the bottom of the excavation.

32 The final preparation step is to compact the soil to provide a solid base for the installation. I used a mechanical plate compactor, but hand tamping also works.

33 To keep the paving blocks in place and in pattern, edging is usually installed around the perimeter. It can be made from treated lumber, bender board, metal or plastic edging strips or even stone products such as bricks set vertically or at an angle in the ground. I chose plastic strip edging because it is easy to work with, anchors well with galvanized landscape spikes, is not affected by weather and virtually disappears when installed. The vertical face of the edging sits against and contains the pavers. The horizontal face rests on the ground and provides lots of holes for anchor spikes. The cutouts make it easy to notch around obstructions. Spike holes line up and interlock to make strong 90° corners.

34 Cutting away edge sections at the outer edge of the cutouts allows the edging to be bent into a gentle curve.

35 With the edging in place, put down a layer of landscape fabric. Cover that with a layer of gravel and rake it evenly. (The landscape fabric will discourage weeds and grass from growing up through the pavers while allowing rain and moisture to drain through.)

36 Next, add a layer of sand and rake it to approximately the proper depth. Then set two pieces of 1"-diameter (25mm) metal electrical conduit in the sand, front to back and about 12" (305mm) in from the outside edges, at the sand finish grade height. Use a 2×4 screed across the tops of the tubing to evenly distribute and level the sand.

37 When the grading and leveling is complete, remove the tubing pieces and fill the resulting impressions with sand to level.

38 With a good multilayered support bed in place, you can begin installing of the pavers. Using batter boards, establish a centerline front to back. (Since you're using three different sizes of blocks, the centerline doesn't directly relate to the pattern distribution, but it gives a good general reference.) I also pull a line side to side across the front two posts to show where the straight sides end and the curved edges begin.

39 Using a random side-to-side pattern, carefully lay the pavers on top of the sand. Experiment with the three different sizes of blocks to determine the best distribution for each row. Continue setting whole blocks — starting at the center and working out toward the edges — past the line where the curved edges begin and out to the front.

40 Once most of the pavers are in place, all you need to do is cut the blocks that must be trimmed to fit within the perimeter. Use a hand-activated block cutter, which snaps the block rather than actually cutting it. There is more waste from miscuts with this method, but it's much more economical that renting a power saw. Also, the snapped edges will be rough — more like the existing edges than those cut with a saw.

41 Now it's time to tamp the blocks into the sand bed to the finish grade level. Sprinkle sand over the entire paver surface. Then use a broom to force it down into the cracks and joints. Seat the pavers using a rented mechanical plate compactor. (You could do the same thing with a wood block and a mallet but it would take longer.) Keep adding more sand as you go over the surface and watch the level of the pavers carefully. The compactor forces the pavers down into the sand bed,and the broomed sand locks them in place.

42 The final step is to add the missing base trim pieces at the bottom of the four posts. Fit the trim and install it with small galvanized box nails. (The trim pieces can be removed and replaced in the future if damage from ground contact occurs.) When soil or mulching material is raked into place against the pavers, the plastic edging disappears. It's time to build something to sit on.

(suppliers)

ABRAXAS CROW COMPANY
Gunter Reimnitz
reimnitz@olypen.com
Port Townsend, WA
360-379-3281
www.abraxascrow.com
Forge/weld/cut/bend steel sculptures

ADAMS & KENNEDY – THE WOOD SOURCE
6178 Mitch Owen Rd.
P.O. Box 700
Manotick, ON
Canada K4M 1A6
613-822-6800
www.wood-source.com
Wood supply

ADJUSTABLE CLAMP COMPANY
404 N. Armour St.
Chicago, IL 60622
312-666-0640
www.adjustableclamp.com
Clamps and woodworking tools

AWPA
American Wood Preservers Association
P.O. Box 361784
Birmingham, AL
205-733-4077
www.awpa.com
Non-profit organization responsible for promulgating voluntary wood preservation

B&Q
B&Q Head Office
Portswood House
1 Hampshire Corporate Park
Chandlers Ford
Eastleigh
Hampshire SO53 3YX
0845 609 6688
www.diy.com
Woodworking tools, supplies and hardware

BETTER BARNS
126 Main Street South
Bethlehem, CT 06751
888-266-1960
www.betterbarns.com
Barns & shed buildings, paans and hardware

CONSTANTINE'S WOOD CENTER OF FLORIDA
1040 E. Oakland Park Blvd.
Fort Lauderdale, FL 33334
800-443-9667
www.constintines.com
Tools, woods, veneers, hardware

COTTAGE HOME NETWORK
Jim Tolpin
www.cottagehome.net
Cottage homes, the people who build them, and a large collection of resources for further exploration

DALY'S
3525 Stone Way North
Seattle, WA 98103
800-735-7019
www.dalyspaint.com
Paint, decorating, interior and exterior wood-finishing products

DEWALT INDUSTRIAL TOOL COMPANY
701 East Joppa Road TW425
Baltimore, MD 21286
800-4DEWALT
www.dewalt.com
Industrial and woodworking tools and accessories

DOWELMAX
O.M.S. Company Ltd.
203 - 814 West15th Street
North Vancouver, B.C.
V7P 1M6 Canada
877-986-9400
www.dowelmax.com
Precesion-engineered dowel joining system

EDENSAW WOODS, LTD.
2111 Seton Road
Port Townsend, WA 98368
800-745-3336
www.edensaw.com
Importers, wholesalers and retailers of domestic and exotic woods, high-quality lumber, plywoods and veneers

FESTOOL USA
Tooltechnic Systems, LLC.
140 Los Carneros Way
Goleta, CA 93117
888-337-8600
www.festoolusa.com
Woodworking and industrial power tools

FRANK PAXTON LUMBER COMPANY
5701 W. 66th St.
Chicago, IL 60638
800-323-2203
www.paxtonwood.com
Wood, hardware, tools, books

HARDWICK'S
4214 Roosevelt Way NE
Seattle, WA 98105
866-369-6525
www.ehardwicks.com
An eclectic family owned and operated hardware and tool store since 1932. The Northwest School of Wooden Boatbuilding takes each entering class on a fieldtrip to Hardwick's to buy their required hand tools

THE HOME DEPOT
2455 Paces Ferry Rd.
Atlanta, GA 30339
800-553-3199 (U.S.)
800-668-0525 (Canada)
www.homedepot.com
Woodworking tools, supplies and hardware

KELLER & CO.
1327 I Street
Petaluma, CA 94952
800-995-2456
www.kellerdovetail.com
The Keller dovetail system offers precision through dovetail router jigs that perform consistently with simplicity, speed and accuracy

KREG TOOL COMPANY
201 Campus Drive
Huxley, IA 50124
800-447-8638
www.kregtool.com
A pioneer in pocket hole joinery technology and precision measuring accessories for woodworking machinery

LEE VALLEY TOOLS LTD.
P.O. Box 1780
Ogdensburg, NY 13669-6780
800-871-8158 (U.S.)
800-267-8767 (Canada)
www.leevalley.com
Woodworking tools and hardware

LOWE'S HOME IMPROVEMENT WAREHOUSE
P.O. Box 1111
North Wilkesboro, NC 28656
800-445-6937
www.lowes.com
Woodworking tools, supplies and hardware

MAKITA U.S.A., INC.
14930 Northam Street
La Mirada, CA 90638
800-4MAKITA
www.makita.com
Industrial and woodworking tools

ROCKLER WOODWORKING AND HARDWARE
4365 Willow Dr.
Medina, MN 55340
800-279-4441
www.rockler.com
Woodworking tools, hardware and books

THE STANLEY WORKS
1000 Stanley Drive
New Britain, CT 06053
860-255-5111
www.stanleyworks.com
Tools and hardware

TOOL TREND LTD.
140 Snow Blvd.
Thornhill, ON
Canada L4K 4L1
416-663-8665
Woodworking tools and hardware

VAUGHAN & BUSHNELL MFG. CO.
11414 Maple Ave.
Hebron, IL 60034
815-648-2446
www.vaughanmfg.com
Hammers and other tools

VINTAGE HARDWARE
2700 Sims Way
Port Townsend, WA 98368
360-379-9030
www.vintagehardware.com
Reproduction vintage antique hardware and lighting from the Victorian, Art Nouveau, Art Deco, Bungalow and Mission Style homes

VERMONT CASTINGS
CFM Corporation
2695 Meadowvale Boulevard
Mississauga, Ontario
L5N 8N3 Canada
800-525-1898
www.vermontcastings.com
Fireplaces, hearths and stoves

WOODCRAFT
406 Airport Industrial Park Rd.
P.O. Box 1686
Parkersburg, WV 26104
800-535-4482
www.woodcraft.com
Woodworking hardware

WOODWORKER'S SUPPLY
1108 North Glenn Rd.
Casper, WY 82601
800-645-9292
http://woodworker.com
Woodworking tools and accessoried, finishing supplies, books and plans

Adirondack-style fanback love-
    seat, 9–21

Barbecue grill, 63
Barbecue station, 58–71
Beam ends, 104–106
Benches
    bench seats, 23–31
    potting bench, 49–57
Braces, 108–113

Concrete
    paving blocks, 118
    for setting posts, 64, 98, 100
Covered BBQ station, 58–71
Curves, 16, 78
Cutoff solution, 77, 79, 107

Decking, 66, 85
Door and garden fence, 35–47

Electrical power
    galvanized metal conduit, 76
    safety note, 39
    trenching, 39, 75
    wet-location conduit, 71

Fasteners
    attaching from below, 31
    avoiding splitting wood, 21
    door and hinge hardware, 47, 93
    fanback loveseat, 13, 14
    for hardwoods, 11
    for pressure-treated wood, 102
Finishing
    cutoff solution, 77, 79, 107
    marine sealer, 21
    oil sealer, 33, 47
    preservative stain, 88
Footprints, 98–99

Garden fence with door, 35–47
Glass shelving, safety tips, 2

Hardware. See Fasteners

Landscape cloth, 65, 76, 85, 123
Loveseat, 9–21
Lumber. See Wood for outdoor
    furniture

Materials
    roofing, 69
    wood. See Wood for outdoor
        furniture
Metric conversion chart, 2
Miter gauge safety, 27

Patterns, 13, 104–105
Paving stones, 117–125
Planning
    covered BBQ station, 62
    outdoor furniture, 25
    tool shed, 84
    trellis, 98
Posts
    cutting to length, 107–108
    pressure-treated, 64, 98
    setting, 64, 98, 100–101, 103
    two-support-post design, 61
Potting bench, 49–57
Power equipment
    cutting decking, 66
    cutting post tops, 107
    cutting saw holes, 105
    miter gauge, 27
    router blowout, 26
    safety tips, 2
    tablesaw, 26
Pressure-treated lumber
    fasteners, 102
    installation, 78
    for paving block edging, 122
    for posts, 64, 98
    safety tips for handling, 102

Roofing, 69–70, 89
Router blowout, 26

Safety tips
    cutting post tops, 107
    cutting saw holes, 105
    electricity, 39
    glass shelving, 2
    miter gauge, 27
    outdoor electrical wiring, 39
    power equipment, 2
    for pressure-treated wood, 102
    tablesaw, 26
Sizing fanback slats, 18
Spacers, 18–20, 31
Suppliers, 126

Table, 23, 31–33
Techtips
    avoid splitting, 21
    construction planning, 25, 98
    fastening hardwoods, 11
    patterns, 104
    router blowout, 26
    two-support-post design, 61
Tool shed, 81–93
Trellis
    beam ends, 104–106
    braces, 109–113
    draining, 115
    paving stones, 117–125
    planning and design, 96–99
    posts, 100–103, 107–108
    side panels, 114
    top trellis pieces, 116
Trenching for electrical lines, 39,
    75

Walkway, 73–79
Window, 91
Wood for outdoor furniture
    Alaska yellow cedar, 9, 13, 21
    cedar, 52, 57, 66
    choices, 9
    cutoff solution, 77, 79, 107
    decking, 66
    dimension lumber, 52
    Douglas fir, 66, 76, 85
    fastening hardwoods, 11
    ipe, 9, 21
    pressure-treated lumber. See
        Pressure-treated lumber
    teak, 9, 23
    tigerwood, 66

(index)

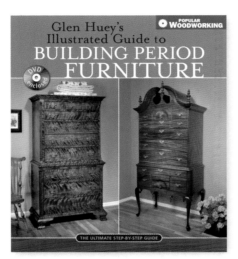
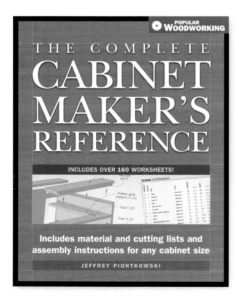